A GUIDE TO SURVIVING YOUTH FOOTBALL

WRITTEN BY ADAM SIBLEY

Title: A Guide to Surviving Youth Football

Author: Adam David Sibley

ISBN: 978-1-4452-0348-5

Publisher: Lulu

All rights reserved. No part of this book may be reproduced or transmitted in any form or by any means, electronic or mechanical, including photocopying, recording or by any information storage and retrieval system, without written permission from the author, except for the inclusion of brief quotations in a review.

Copyright © Adam Sibley 2009

First Edition, 2009

Acknowledgements

This book would have not been possible without the love and support of family, friends and all the people that I have worked with in football. I have had the pleasure of meeting some great people and characters during my time in football which have made the experience all that more enjoyable. My time in football has already given me a lifetime of memories which I will never forget.

I need to thank Ray Brown who trained me to be a Football Referee at the age of twelve. He was my mentor and supported me through my early years in refereeing.

He arranged for me to referee at some great games and places including school finals and England Schoolboy trials. The referees around Cornwall and the leagues I officiated in were always so supportive of me for which I will always be thankful for.

A huge thanks has to go to Tony and Julia Gorski who not only took me in to the family which was their youth football club (Liskeard Junior Football Club) but also in to their own family. After starting off as a referee for them they took me in to the fold and got me on courses to get my coaching qualifications. They then put me in touch with the coaches of all the teams within the club so I could get some experience. They are always interested in what I am doing and are always trying to support me in any way they can. In football you meet many acquaintances but few friends so I am so glad to have great friends I have met through football. If you can work with friends in football it makes the experience that much better.

I need to thank Simon Truscott who brought me in as an assistant coach with his under 13 Liskeard team and for two seasons let me get some hands on experience in what turned in to a real education in youth football. I will always remember what I learnt in those two seasons and take the memories with me.

Since my two seasons there I have been lucky enough to get a different experience working with Ian Woodhouse and our new girls' team. To be a great youth coach you need experience in working with all age groups as well as working with both boys and girls and if it wasn't for Ian I wouldn't have had that experience so a huge thanks has to go to him.

Last but by no means least I have to give a shout out to my coaching guru and inspiration Rhys Sullivan. The son of a great coach Rhys has coaching running through his blood. He has made his passion in to his career gaining his UEFA B qualification and flying across the globe to work in various states across America as a youth football coach alongside working with a professional club when he is in the UK. He dedicates himself to becoming the best coach he can be, constantly studying, learning and practicing. If you need feedback or new ideas he is always ready to lend a helping hand. He knows how to get the best out of players and already has people singing his praises on both sides of the Atlantic.

I know there are lots of people I have missed out here but to name you all would probably take two hundred pages. In short thanks to everybody that has come on the journey with me and thanks to all those who have supported me over the years in football it means a lot.

Contents

9 Introduction

14 Acquiring Players

24 Pre-Season Build Up

31 Training

40 Fundraising

49 Leagues

55 Home Games

65 Away Games

75 Facilities

83 Referees

93 Opposing Managers

98 Parents

109 Stars in their Eyes

120 Winning at all Costs

127 Assistant Coaches

131 Coaching Family Members

136 Counsellor, Childminder, Mentor, Friend and Parent all Rolled in to One.

142 Getting Emotional

148 Being the Best You Can Be

154 Arguing Players

159 Paperwork and the Media

165 Politics

172 Getting Involved With the Club

176 Presentation Evening and Rewarding Your Players

182 Leadership

188 For the Love of the Game

193 Final Thoughts

Introduction

So you want to become a youth football coach do you? You've seen other people do it, you've been following football for years and you think you would make a good coach. You may want to become a football coach to give back to the community. You may be doing it because you love working with young people. You may be doing it because you have a child you want to coach, or it may just be something you saw on TV and thought it would be nice to do. Whatever your reason for wanting to do it this book is for you. The more great coaches we can help in to football the better, as these young people need you.

When thinking about coaching youth football there are a lot of things you need to be aware of. Some of these things you may not have thought of and that is where this book comes in. After years spent in youth football I have compiled this book as a dossier of all the things you need to be aware of and able to do if you want to become a great youth football coach.

Normally when you start in youth football you have to work a lot of things out for yourself or learn by trial and error. No matter how many courses you go on or how many people you speak to it can't quite prepare you for the reality of youth football. That is what I am trying to do for you with this book. This book will discuss the things which people may not talk about, or not think about, as well as taking you through the qualities it takes to be a great youth football coach.

The experience when you first become a youth football coach can be quite overwhelming as there is so much to do but don't fear as this book is here to help you prepare and be ready for it. Chapter by chapter I will be breaking down areas of youth football you need to be aware of and how to deal with those areas. Whether it be dealing with parents, running training sessions, or getting your team registered it's all in here and more.

So many people go in to football coaching blind or with rose tinted glasses on and when they see the realities for themselves it can scare them off. The point of this book is to educate and inform would-be coaches in an effort to help stop coaches starting teams or starting coaching and then quitting mid-way through a season or only a short time into their career as a youth football coach.

There are also a great many people in the country with coaching qualifications they aren't using. If you fall in to this category I hope this book can inspire you to want to get involved again in coaching youth football.

Being a youth football coach is one of the most amazing things you can do with your life and it can provide you with a lifetime worth of happy memories. This book is aimed to try and help you get that with your team and your career in coaching, to make sure you get those memories and to help you get the most out of your coaching.

If you already are a coach or are a retired coach I hope this book will provide you with some amusement and stir back your own memories. I am sure you will find many similarities with your own time in coaching and youth football with the stories and information I share in this book. Or if you are reading this book purely for entertainment, research or reference purposes I hope you find it an enjoyable read.

If you are about to become a coach you will have the enthusiasm and the big ideas that every new coach has and needs to have to make an impact in the youth coaching world. Now you need to read the book to be sure that your ideas aren't misguided and that you have enough enthusiasm to put up with all the hassle and problems which can come with being a youth football coach.

Being a new football coach is an exciting time. Nothing beats your first training session and you will always remember your first game regardless of what the score is and where it is played. That first goal, that first win, that first season, there is nothing like it. My purpose in this book in arming you with all the information you need isn't about trying to put you off being a youth coach it is about making sure you are going to enjoy your experience no matter what happens or how things go. The positives in youth football coaching outweigh the negatives and armed with the right information and the right enthusiasm you will be able to handle those negatives with ease.

This book is for every coach regardless of what stage you are at in your career or what stage you are at with your team. Whether your team hasn't been formed yet or if you have been coaching for more years than you care to remember this book is for you.

So read on and find out what awaits you in youth football coaching, what you have to look forward to and how you can handle any situation which is thrown your way.

Acquiring Players

When you are starting a new team one of the most important tasks you will face is player recruitment. There is no point trying to start a team if there isn't enough interest or demand. You don't want to be having to convince players or twist their arms to play football. You need a group of players that want to play football; and want to play for your team. So before you start a team you need to make sure that the demand is there.

Once you have established that demand is there you then need to start getting players signed up. You can do this in many ways. Most youth football teams are started by a small nucleus of friends who then manage to get their other friends to join. If you've got a team full of friends this is a good start. They will all get on and know each other but you need to remember you aren't starting a youth social club. You want players there who want to play football and aren't just doing it so that they can hang out with their friends. On top of this if you have a team of friends you have to remember that when good friends fall out with each other the fallout can be even worse than if just two team mates have a serious disagreement. If you have a team of friends and two of them fall out it may force the rest to pick sides and that could create a division within your team.

The way most coaches go about getting players is through local advertising and press. They will contact the local press and ask if they can announce details about the team and training. They will then start putting up flyers and posters with all the information on in schools, local youth organizations and community notice boards.

Another common way is to hold an open trial where you invite players from all around to try out at a one off session and then based on who performs well the coach will decide who to take on. This is a practice which is normally done by academy and centre of excellence teams. If you have an open trial and not many players show up then it becomes a pointless exercise as it means you have to take them all on and will still need to find more players from somewhere.

If after advertising you aren't getting enough players in then you have to start digging deeper to uncover talent. This is where you need to start talking to P.E staff at your local schools to see if they can get the word out. It's always good to get in touch with your league or your local FA and see if they have any suggestions or ways in which they can help. You can also start looking at young people in your age bracket that play other sports as they may be interested in taking up football and there may be skills that they have learnt in their sport which they can bring over to football. Failing this if your team is part of a big club then you need to speak to all the teams and find out if players in the other teams have relatives or friends that would be interested in joining your team.

When signing players you have to know beforehand what you are looking for in a player. Is it their attitude or their skill level which is most important? When looking at players take a list of what criteria are essential and which are desirable in a player and tick them off as you see them so you can get a quick snapshot of where the player is at. Remember to always get more players than you need as during the season you may lose a few.

Once you find a player you like you need to get them signed up as quickly as possible. So as soon as you have made the decision you need to give the player the forms that they and their parents will need to fill out along with a list of things that you need from them. Make sure you have the forms with you at all times, and make sure you get them to the player as quickly possible. The longer you leave it before getting the form to the player the greater the chance of another team signing them or them missing the cut-off date for registrations before the season starts. Once the player has the form you need to keep chasing them up about it. Get all the information back as quickly as possible because if you only see your players on a weekly basis, by the player not getting the form ready in time for training it could mean two or more weeks before you see that form.

Sometimes it is good to give the forms to the parent if they are around. By doing this you make sure that the parent knows what's going on and you speed up the process. If they aren't around and the player is taking some time with their forms don't be afraid to ring the parents or pay them a visit. Doing this will also make the parents more comfortable with you which will make the player more likely to be able to sign, and sign quickly as some parents won't put pen to paper until they have spoken to or met with the coaches. If a player says they want to join your team you need to get them to commit, it is all well and good having them train each week saying that they want to join but without the signed forms they are no good to you.

If you want to get your entire player signing done at the same time then you need to hold a signing-on night. This is where you tell all the players you want to sign to attend a venue at a time where you will be waiting to go through all their paperwork. If you just give forms to players and let them go away then you may get the forms back in drips and drabs so by doing it this way you can get it all done in one night. When telling players about the signing-on night you also need to tell them what they need to bring with them. Now you will still get players who won't attend or won't bring all the things they need to the signing-on night but if you can get the bulk of the work done in one night then it leaves you with only a few to chase after.

When selecting players you need to make sure you have the right balance of players in all positions. If you don't then you need to be sure that you can convert your players and get them to play in positions that they didn't come to play in. You can't have a team full of strikers or full of defenders. If you don't have balance and you can't get players to change positions then you are in a very tricky situation.

You need a lot of different styles of footballer in your team; if they are all the same and play in the same way then they won't be versatile as a team. You need midfielders that can win the ball and you need attacking midfielders that can turn defence in to attack. You need left footers as well as right footers; you need strong players and quick players. It's all about finding the right blend.

It's not all about finding the best players and signing them up. It's about finding players that you can turn in to the best players as that is your job as a coach. It's about finding players that will listen to you and then do as you ask of them. It's about finding players that do the basics and keep it simple without all the flashy tricks, players that just go in there and get the job done. Most important of all though you need team players who don't have egos and aren't greedy with the ball.

If you already have a team that have been playing in a league you will still need to re-register the players for your next season. The quicker you get this done after the season is over the better as the longer you leave it the bigger the chance there is of your players joining another team. The best thing to do is to get their forms signed and in before the last game of the season and before they go away for their summer holidays. This may not be possible as it depends on when your league make the forms available to you; some leagues won't make them available until some time after the season has finished. But regardless, if you can, you should.

If you are coaching a team that you have already had for at least a season you will know what your team is lacking or what it needs so you can use that information to decide what you want to bring in. You may decide that even though you need something extra, bringing in another player will disrupt the harmony of the team so these are important decisions you need to make.

You have to be prepared that at the end of each season all of your players may not re-sign with the team. They may go to other clubs, they may stop playing, they may move. This is why it is always important to talk to your players and the parents of your players about where they stand in regards to the new season. The news of some players leaving may come out of the blue but some players and parents will let you know what they are thinking.

The worst thing about re-signing players is having to tell some players you are not re-signing them. Just because a player signed with you last season it is still up to you as the coach whether to sign them or not for next season. In a way it is the easiest time to do it after the season has finished and before the new season starts as it will cause the least amount of distraction to your team. When doing this you will know that they have to go, you know it is the right decision for the team as they may have become too disruptive or not playing as you want them to, but it doesn't make it easy. If you want to bring in new players you have to let some of your existing players go to make room for them. You can't just keep signing players without losing some as you will end up not being able to give enough of your players a good amount of game time.

Sometimes you have to gamble on new players. You may have to judge and decide on a player after only seeing them perform once or twice. If you only see them in training you don't know what they are like in a game situation in which that player may not look as good. It is also hard to judge someone's attitude after only a couple of viewings. When a player comes to try out or when they know you are watching them they will be doing their best to impress but once they have got signed you may see a completely different player. It's easy to change your attitude for a couple of games but you can't keep that up throughout a season and eventually your true character will out.

As a coach you have to make decisions and you aren't always going to make the right decision but you have to live with it. If you are left with a team which hasn't got the right blend of players then it is up to you as a coach to roll your sleeves up and sort it out. That's when you find out how good a coach you really are. If you can turn a striker in to a defender or if you can get your worst behaved player and turn them in to your best behaved player then you can judge how good you are as a coach.

When it comes down to behaviour you have to decide whether a player with bad behaviour is worth the effort of trying to turn around. You have to be able to see the potential in them and make a decision based on that. You have to decide whether it's worth the disruption to the rest of the team to bring them in for what you are going to get out of it. If you think you can turn them around you have to try and figure out how many weeks you are going to have where training is disrupted before you get their behaviour sorted and if that period is going to be too long or not.

As a coach you have to be in control of which players you bring in. You need to be sure that bringing them in is in the best interests of the team. You will get many players wanting to bring their friends in or parents who want their children to play for your team, but every player in your team should be there because they deserve their place and not because they have got there through their network of friends and contacts.

Pre-Season Build Up

The pre-season is the most important time for any team. If you are keeping the same team from last season it is your first chance to assess where they are at with their fitness and skills since the Spring / Summer break from football.

The date you set for the start of pre-season is very important as you need to give your players a big enough break from football but you need to get them back early enough to make sure you hit the ground running at the beginning of the season. If you are continuing with a team it is important to set and announce the date that pre-season will start before your players go on their post-season break so everyone is aware of it.

As a coach you have to be aware that your players will go away with their families over the summer break but you can't wait for everyone to get back from holiday to start training. With this in mind you have to set a date knowing that you will be missing some of your players on some weeks but as long as you can get the majority of the team together on a weekly basis you can get some work done.

Regardless of whether it's a new team you are starting, or a team you are carrying on with, pre-season is a time to look at what you are missing and if you need to bring in any extra players. It's the time where you assess where you are weak and where you need to improve.

Fitness should be the major focus of your pre-season training. Some of your players won't have done too much sport over the holidays, they may have been doing a lot of TV watching and playing on computer games. It is important that by the time the first game comes around they are fit enough to last a full game so training sessions over the first few weeks will consist of a lot of running and conditioning work.

Before you start pre-season you should have a plan of what you want to cover each week and know what level you want your players to be at by the time the first game comes around. This season you may want to test out new tactics, new formations, or players in new positions. This is your time to do this as if you want players to play in different positions for you during the rest of the season they need to be comfortable playing in them.

Pre-season is where you as a coach should be setting out what you expect from your players this season and telling them what you want to achieve. It is a time to make sure everyone's attitude is right, and a time to see who really wants to play for the team. During this time some players may quit on you or you may have to get rid of some players and this is why it is always good to start off with a few more players than you need in pre-season training. This allows your team to handle losing a few players without their dismissal hurting the team.

From your first training session of the season you should tell and show your players what behaviour and attitude you will accept and what you won't tolerate. You have to have a hard line and stick to it. The minute you let one player get away with backchat or misbehaving is the minute they will start misbehaving even more and other players will notice this and think they can misbehave. It's easier to drill it in to them from the start and to keep that hard line than trying to pull them back in to line after letting them misbehave. The hardest thing but the most important thing to win and to have is your players respect. Without it you will have problems every season that you coach your team.

As well as organising weekly training sessions you need to also arrange friendlies. The quicker you can arrange friendly matches the better as other coaches will also be ringing around to arrange friendlies. If you want your pick of who to play you have to get in there early. The choices you make on who to play in friendlies are important so you need to think strategically about it.

In pre-season you don't want your players to pick up injuries so you don't want to play a team who are known for being overly physical. You want a combination of games which once complete will have given every position on your team a workout and enough minutes to look at all your squad. By the end of your friendlies you also need the players who you think will be your starting players next season to be match fit.

Through your friendlies you want your players to be confident but not over-confident so you want to play teams with a range of abilities. If you play all your friendlies against better teams it's going to affect your team's confidence but if you just play against teams that are weaker than you then your team can get over-confident and think they are better than what they are. If your team doesn't think they are any good they will stop trying and if your team think they are better than what they are they will stop putting one hundred percent in.

Another big decision is the number of games you play, you don't want to overwork your players before the season but you need to make sure they are ready. This will vary from team to team and there is no magic number but you need be prepared to cancel or add friendlies at last minute depending on how your team is getting on.

An important decision you need to make with your friendlies is do you play against teams you are going to be playing against in the upcoming season. By playing friendlies against teams from your league it can give you a good chance to look at their players and their tactics but on the same token it gives your opponents the chance to do exactly the same thing. You need to decide if it is that important to have a look at them and if it is worth the risk of them being able to work out your team and your tactics. If you are playing in a new league against teams you have never played before it can be more important to play them in friendlies than if you are playing in the same league this season as last season. You want your team to be confident against every team they play against and at every ground they go to so if you are joining a new league and playing a friendly against a team in your league and it helps your players' confidence then it could be a wise decision to get it arranged.

The results of the friendlies don't matter. What matters is what your players learn and gain from each game. It's confidence and fitness which is key, everything else is a bonus.

By the end of pre-season you should know what your players are capable of and in what positions they will excel in. Your team should know each others names and how they like to play the game. Each one of your players should be confident playing in the same team with each other and everybody should be willing to put in one hundred and ten percent in every game for the team.

During the first league game of the season you will be able to see which teams did their pre-season right and who didn't. This is where you get the reward for all the hard work. To me pre-season is all about the basics and getting the fundamentals right. Your pre-season training develops a strong base. As the season goes on you can build in fancy skills and complicated tactics to your game but none of this is possible if your players can't do and can't master the basics of football and playing football in a team.

Training

As a coach your training sessions will be one of the most important times of the week. Training is where you get your players ready for your next game and where you help mould them in to better players. You will normally only get one training session a week which lasts for one hour so you have to make the most of it.

Training is also a time where you have to get important information over to your players like details for the next game, where you are going to meet and what time you are going to meet. It is where you need to get your players focused and paying attention.

During the later Spring, Summer and early Autumn you will usually train on grass and you will have sunlight until late in the evening. These training sessions can be good as you aren't as tight for time as if you had booked on to an Astroturf surface so if you are running behind on your schedule you can extend your training session at no extra cost and still in daylight. As you play your league games on grass the more time you can spend training on grass the better. The only problem can be with the great British weather you need to make sure your players bring the right footwear depending on the weather and conditions. If the weather is torrential it may mean you have to cancel training if you are on grass whereas the benefit of Astroturf is that you can play on it in any weather.

If the weather is good, training in the summer is a good test as the players will also have the heat to deal with during pre-season training which will help them get fit and lose any extra pounds as they sweat through pre-season fitness regimes. It will get colder as autumn draws in and in the few weeks before you switch over to Astroturf you will also have to deal with fading light which will get even earlier each week leaving you with little training time or having to train in the dark.

When it comes time to switch to Astroturf you will no longer have the luxury of having extra training time and being the only team using a huge pitch. Normally most astroturfs are heavily booked and you are only allowed the hour you paid for and no more. So when you get to the Astroturf for your session you will normally have to kick off the group that was on there before you who have overrun which will cut in to your time and then at the end the next group who are on after you will come early and hang around the pitch before trying to get on as early as possible. On Astroturf you will normally get a smaller pitch than you are use to on grass so everyone will be on top of each other and you will have less space to work with.

To have a good training session it takes a lot of pre planning. You need to plan the session and have a goal of what you want to have achieved by the end of the session. Planning also means making sure you have all the equipment you need and that everything you have is in the proper condition like pumping up balls, washing bibs etc. As a coach you should set the example by being the first person to get to training, if you are coaching out on the grass you can set up early but if you are on an Astroturf you need to get on there as quickly as possible so not to lose too much time setting up your equipment.

When planning always have short term and long term goals. Each training session needs to be used to get ready for the next game but you also need to develop your players towards a long term goal of the level you want them to be at. Each drill you do should be geared towards achieving those goals. You need to be prepared to adapt throughout the season when you notice things your team needs to work on then you need to build them in to training. As well as looking at the team as a whole be sure to look at every player individually as each player will have different needs and different things they need to improve on. As well as having drills for the whole team you need to also design individual drills for different players or different sets of positions as there are things the goalkeeper needs to learn which the midfield don't and so on.

When working with young people the first ten minutes of training will be a nightmare as they all tend to come to training in a hyperactive state. They will have been cooped up in school all day and they won't have seen some of their team mates all week so will want to catch up. As a coach you need to get them back in line as quickly as possible and focused on training. This is why warming up is so important as not only does it get the body ready it gets the players minds focused on the rest of training.

Young people like to question everything so every time you explain a new drill you will get players asking you why they have to do it and what are they getting out of it. Players always think they know best and think they are too good to do drills you set up so it is up to you to get them to do them, do them properly and learn what they are getting out of it. If you let the players dictate to you once what you are going to do then they will be trying to dictate for the rest of the season and just doing what they please. If you ask a player what they want to do nine times out of ten they will say a match but just having matches every week at training isn't going to help them learn and develop. Having a game for a small part of training can be a good thing as long as it is done in a controlled way and you as a coach are dictating like playing games where players can only take two touches or encouraging them to get it wide and get crosses in.

If you don't have an assistant coach trying to manage your whole squad in training can be hard. All it takes is for one of your players to be having a bad week to bring down everyone around them. If a player is out of line you have to step on it as quickly as possible but in a way which doesn't stop others from training as if you spend too long trying to sort out one player it affects the time you have for the rest of the team.

Players are more likely to mess around in training than on a game day. When you are at training the game seems so far away from training and many players don't stop to think that you may base your decision on who is going to play in the game on who does well in training.

The important thing to do in training is to not talk too much. If you only have a short amount of time it is more important that your players get time on the ball rather than talking about it. So save your big talks for after training or for before and after games. If you are doing a lot of talking the players will become disinterested, disruptive and switch off to what you are saying. Explain the drills and what you are doing but let your players get on with it without trying to over explain it. Then when you have a drill in progress you can go round individually to players and coach them whilst they are doing drills.

To stop your players from wondering and misbehaving design drills so that everyone is involved all the time. Try to avoid exercises where only one or two players are active at anyone time with the rest watching or waiting for their turn. Have drills which involve the whole group or exercises where you have one ball per player or one ball between two. Training should be about getting all your players as much time on the ball as possible and being as active as possible.

Training is where you build discipline into your team. If you want your players to respect you and listen to you during games its training where you win that attention and respect. If you don't have respect and attention for match days it makes your job that much harder. Training is about getting your team into a routine. A regime, if you will. Young people need routine in order to dedicate themselves to something and to focus on it.

The parents of your players may want to come and watch training. Now as a coach that's your call whether or not you let them stay or encourage them to stay. Some coaches like the players to have no distractions whereas some like to see the support shown by the parents and think it will give the players a boost. Whichever way you decide it has to be one rule for everybody with no exceptions.

When setting your training day and time be sure to choose a day and time where you can get the most players at training. If you know your players or potential players do other activities on a set evening don't put your training there. You will never be able to please everybody but you need to get the most amount of people to training as possible. If you want to run a hard line and test your players desire to play football then you can schedule it for the same night as they have other activities making them choose which one they want to do. If you do this you have to be prepared for some of your players to choose another activity over football. Some coaches like their players to have other activities and some like them to be focused on football so again that's your call.

When you have decided on a time for training don't change it. If you change it once then you're more likely to change it again and everybody will want their say on what night it should be on. Like I say, with training you are never going to please everybody but as the coach you need to be firm that when a day and time is set it's stuck to. If you use a facility like an Astroturf which isn't owned by the club and is a busy facility then you may not have the luxury of choosing a time and day and you may just have to take what they have. If it is a busy facility and if there is a specific day and time you want the facility you need to be booking a year in advance to maximise your chance of guaranteeing the slot.

As a coach if you are unsure of how to run a training session go and have a look at how others are doing it and take the bits you like and incorporate them in to your training. I personally like to look at what professional clubs and other youth clubs are doing. I will also look at other sports for tips on different training methods and fitness regimes which you can adapt for football. The key thing is finding what works for your team and then if it's not broke don't try and change it. Keep up to date on the latest training methods but be aware that what is considered good or bad and right or wrong to do in training will change on a regular basis. If you paid attention to all of these changes it would see you changing techniques every week. The key is to be aware but to do what you think is best for the team and trying to stick to it and not be forever changing it.

Fundraising

It may not be the Premiership but running a youth football club is an expensive business. Each year the cost of running a youth team seems to go up and up. No longer is it the case of just turning up to a pitch and playing football with some old kits a bucket of water and a magic sponge.

Before you start a team you need to have insurance which doesn't come cheap. You then need to pay any fees required to register with your local FA and your local league. This is even before you have kicked a ball because without any of these you can't play football.

You then need to acquire somewhere to train and somewhere to play games. If you are playing in Britain during the winter for training you are going to need to book an all weather pitch with floodlights which won't come cheap - especially when you are training every week. Then if you don't own a pitch you may need to hire one or help pay for the upkeep of a pitch if you are using it.

Once you have a home pitch and somewhere to train you will need training equipment and a first aid bag. To do a proper training session you will need things like balls, cones and bibs. Depending on how you want to run training there is a ton of different training equipment you can buy but again that's even more money. To have a proper first aid bag can also be very expensive these days and a correctly stocked first aid bag is a necessity in the world of insurance and claims that we live in. No longer can you just tell a player to run it off when they get hurt.

Due to the cost of equipment it is important you instil a respect of your equipment in your players and any visiting team that uses your equipment. You need to make your equipment last as long as possible and to keep it in top condition for as long as possible. Equipment can get easily damaged if you don't instil that respect and if equipment does get damaged it means you have to find even more money.

Some leagues and clubs will only let you get involved with the club as a coach if you have your coaching certificate, a first aid certificate and a CRB certificate for working with young people. All these cost money to obtain and if your league or club require them then you can't start without them.

Next step is that you need a kit, if you're lucky you may get a kit handed down to you but even if you do there may be bits of kit which are damaged or missing which you need to replace. Even the most basic and cheapest kit is still expensive and to play in a league you will need a kit of some description. Most people fund a kit by getting a sponsor. In return for paying for the kit the sponsor will get their name or company emblazoned on the kit as well as the good PR they get for helping out sport in the community. If you ask players they like playing in new kits and don't like wearing old kits that other teams have worn especially if they are tatty or look like a kit out of the nineteen eighties.

Getting a sponsor for a sports team can be quite challenging as there will be dozens, perhaps even hundreds of other youth sport teams in your area, and probably not the same amount of companies who would be willing to sponsor a youth sport team. Trying to get a sponsor can be very time consuming and soul destroying; getting knock back after knock back. This is why you need to think ahead if you are thinking of running a team and try and get your sponsor in place before your first training starts. Normally most sponsors at local youth clubs are friends or relations of the coach or players so don't be afraid to ask any business owner you know. The only problem which comes from getting a players relative to sponsor the club is that the situation could put pressure on you to play their child when they may not be the right player for that game, to make them captain or to never sub them off as if they pull out of funding then it will leave your team looking for money again so going down this route should always be a last resort.

If you are lucky your sponsor may help by paying for your other costs like fees and training equipment. In youth football other non-essential items which have turned in to must haves are training kits, tracksuits and bags for each player. These items should be way down your list of priorities of what you are looking to raise money for but if you have a sponsor who is willing to pay for them they do make your team look even more professional which will have a positive affect on their attitude and the way the team is perceived by others.

If you run a 7-a-side team then you will need to purchase a set of mini-soccer goals. For what you get, these things can be very expensive. I think one day I may have to set up a business making them! The bill for a set normally runs in to hundreds of pounds and without them you can't play a game of football. To add to this you will also need to purchase some corner flags. It's not just the cost of these items but the storage of them which is the problem as you will either have to pay for some storage or try and borrow someone else's storage space. More often than not coaches have to store them in their garage. With all this kit and equipment you have to look after it well because if it gets damaged or lost that's again more money you have to fork out.

There are lots of costs involved in football which you don't even realise you are spending out for. As a coach most nights you will be on the phone to players, coaches, parents, leagues and venues. You have got the petrol costs of going to training every week and games on the weekends. You also have the washing costs especially if you wash the entire team kit every week. Some clubs will make the players families wash the kit, some will pay for a launderette service and at some clubs the coaches will do all the washing.

On top of all your outgoings you will need a contingency fund for other costs during the season for things like fines, extra travel as well as new or unexpected costs. If you get an unexpected cost during the season and you don't have the money for it, it could put an end to your season so you always need to be prepared for anything.

There are many ways you can raise money including sponsored events, auctions, raffles, donations etc. To raise money you have to be proactive and get off your backside. Raising money can be one of the hardest things to do and I know some people struggle asking other people for money and raising funds but it is a necessity in the current youth football world. You can't rely on sponsors for all your money because if a sponsor pulls out you then need to replace that money somehow. Across the globe just about everything imaginably possible to raise funds has been tried but the key thing to remember is to do something which doesn't require too much investment from the club. The last thing you want to do is lose money when you're trying to raise funds. When thinking about carrying out a fundraising event find out what has worked and what hasn't in the local area. When fundraising you have a team of players who have a whole bunch of relatives and friends so you have an audience there and you need to try and encourage them to donate to the club. These should be your bread and butter as far as raising funds is concerned and then from there you can go out in to the wider community.

As well as fundraising there may be funds and grants you can tap in to. Be sure to speak with your local councils, sports organisations and funding agencies. If you are no good at fundraising then this can be another way of getting some money into you team, it just normally means a lot of form filling. The thing with applying for grants and funds is that you know how much you are going to get in advance - unlike fundraising when you can never be too sure how much you are going to make. As well as local funding organisations there are a lot of national funding projects for youth football and youth sport so don't be afraid to look further afield.

If you can't get organisations to sponsor you or give you grants, try and get services and products in kind. Just because someone or some company can't give you money it doesn't mean that they couldn't give you some free footballs or the free use of a launderette for instance.

Money is always king but over time free services and equipment like this can take a financial burden off the club.

In most clubs the parents of players will help you pay for a lot of the running costs through their payment of annual fees which are set at the beginning of the season and without them you wouldn't be able to keep the club running. However every time costs go up it then leaves you having to either raise more money or bring the cost of fees up but by doing this you may price families out of football which is what you are trying your best not to do. When fundraising you have to be very careful not to rely on your players parents to put their hands in their pockets too often as they already will pay a substantial sum every year.

As a coach you will always see things which you would like to have for your club regardless of how many things you already have and how much money you have in the account. They key is to manage your money sensibly and not just rush out and get things as if you have that mindset then every week you are going to want to rush out and get the next big thing. Before you think of buying all these extras you first have to make sure you have the money to cover all your costs for the season. Then when you have reached that sum then, and only then, can you even consider buying non-essential items but it's worth remembering that you have to start thinking about next season and keeping money in reserve for the new campaign.

Normally as a coach you will have to put your hand in your own pocket on numerous occasions which you don't mind doing as you want your players to have the best of everything but you can't let it get to the stage where you are paying for everything. No team can be run financially sensibly with all the costs being covered by one person. Personally I think it builds character in your team if they don't have the best of everything and have to make do and adapt to equipment and a playing area which may not be perfect. Players need to learn how to make the best of what they have and adapt to situations. If everything is just given to them they just expect it but if they have to work for and earn some new equipment or new kit then it will mean more to them and they will take more care with it.

Leagues

Deciding what league your team should play in can be a tricky decision to make especially if there are lots of leagues in your area to choose from. If you only have one league in your area then your decision will be a lot easier. However, if your local league isn't up to scratch you may still want to look at playing in leagues from outside your area even if it means travelling. If you're not prepared to travel then you will need to try and get some support to form a new league although this will involve a lot of work and will be very time consuming.

Joining a league isn't always as straight forward as you would like to think. You will usually need to apply to join the league and then the members of the league will vote on whether to accept your application. To be able to apply to be a member the league may have certain criteria which you need to fulfil before you can even apply. This means you need to start preparing months before a season is due to start to make sure you are registered in time to join the league. Sometimes if not enough teams register their interest in playing in a league then a league may not be set up for your team's age group so, again, it is important you register your interest as early as possible.

Once you have jumped through all these hoops the league will usually expect a joining fee which you will have to find before they will issue you with a handbook containing all of their rules and regulations. When all of that is done it's time to start registering your players. Most leagues will require you to register all your players by a certain date to be able to play at the start of the season. Player registration will be different in different leagues but it can consist of form filling, getting photos of your players, and getting proof of age for all your players. All of this information will need to be handed to the league by a certain date and in a certain way or else they may hold up your registration or hand down a fine. If your players aren't registered in time for your first league game then your game may be postponed and you may be docked points or again fined.

Some leagues will require you to attend monthly meetings; these will be a time where the board of the league can give you all the latest news updates and where you can bring up matters arising or problems you may be having. This means you will have to give up another evening every month for football related matters.

The league will arrange fixture lists for your league and it is then your duty to make sure your games are played. After every match you will have to send in a signed match report form with the result on and you will have to send in postponement reports if a game is postponed.

If you want to take on a player from another club or one of your players wants to join another club you will have to fill out a transfer form. If a team doesn't want to lose a player they may hold up their transfer which means you have to go even longer without them playing in your team as without that signed form being seen by the league the player won't be able to play for your team. If you play a player who isn't registered to your club it could mean that the result for that match will be null and voided, you may receive a fine or even worse you may get docked points.

Yes, it's just like the professional leagues. In youth football teams don't want to lose their best players – especially not to their rivals - so they will do anything they can to get in the way of it. If you are trying to get a player from a team which you have problems with or are rivals with they may hold it up just to annoy you. You would think that getting a player who is already registered in the league would be quicker and easier than registering a player who hasn't ever played in the league but in reality this isn't always the case.

As a coach you want to try and keep the people who run your league onside. If you make enemies of the people that run the league then it can make your job that much harder as the league can take their time doing your paperwork, hold up transfers and make your fixture list as tricky as possible. Being a coach is stressful enough without making problems for yourself. I'm not saying that all leagues are like this as most are run without these things affecting the football but it's not worth risking it especially if you are new to a league.

If you have a problem with how your league is handling you and your team then you need to go to your local FA for support, advice and guidance. The only problem with doing this is that the people who sit on the board of your league may have involvement or connections with people inside the local FA so you can never be too sure what will happen to your complaint. As well as the teams the league are also registered to the local FA so the local FA have an equal duty to support players, teams and leagues.

If you aren't enjoying the league you are in then the best thing to do is to find another league. If you have a personality clash with people inside the league then you can wait until they step down, but of course there are no guarantees if or when this will happen and you could be waiting forever.

As a coach you will either want to challenge your players and make them the best they possibly can be by playing against the best teams possible or you will be all about winning trophies and if this is the case you will be looking for the easiest league as possible. There may possibly be a promotion structure within your local youth football scene where if you win a league you can get promoted to another or there may not be and if this is the case you will have to apply to join a different league. If there is no league hierarchy then deciding on the best league just comes down to personal opinion.

One problem that can happen when you get promoted to a higher league or join a perceived better league is for some of your best players to leave you. Unlike the contracts which lock players in to professional clubs, in local youth football players can quit or leave your team without any warning and if you lose a handful of players you can go from world beaters one year to bottom of the league the next. When you go up to a better league it is a challenge even if you keep hold of your best players but if you lose them it becomes an even bigger challenge. The more teams you play against the greater the chance that other clubs are going to come in for your players.

Home Games

As a coach when you have a home game you are in charge. If you are in a league where it's up to the home manager to dictate kick off time and day then you are completely in control of everything, but even if you are in a league which dictates kick off days and times then you still have a lot of control and responsibility over what happens.

As a home manager you are not only the point of contact for your own team and their families but you are the point of contact for the away team. If the team visiting you has never been to your ground before, they may ring you up for directions before the game but then they still may get lost on the way so it will be up to you to have your mobile on so you can help direct them.

When the away team gets to your ground it is then your responsibility to introduce yourself and welcome them and show them to any facilities you may have. If you don't have any facilities players and parents may ask you where the nearest toilets or the nearest shop is so you need to know your local area.

As a home manager it is up to you to show understanding if an away team is running late due to traffic or getting lost and delay the time of kick off to allow the opposition to have a proper warm up and not miss the kick off. If you decide not to delay the kick off which is still your right you can expect the same treatment when you go away to teams. You'd better not be late or get lost going to any away games if you decide to go down this route!

As the home manager it is up to you to monitor the pitch in the week building up to the game, checking that it is in a playable state whilst keeping an eye on the weather forecast. If you are using a pitch which doesn't belong to you, you need to also make sure that it has been booked and that no one else is using the pitch at that time. It is the home manager's call whether a game is postponed or not. If the home manager deems the pitch to be unplayable or the weather too bad to play in then they can call the game off. It is normally the kind thing to do to keep your opposing manager in the loop if the game looks like it may be unplayable and to let them know at the earliest convenience if the game is to be postponed. If you are going to postpone a game you have to figure out when the away team would be leaving so you can let them know before they set off but still give the pitch and the weather as much time to improve as possible. To travel all the way for an away game to find out it has been called off is very frustrating so again if you don't want that happening to you don't do it to anyone else.

If you are a win-at-all-costs coach and you have the power to dictate the kick off time and day you will pick a time and day that is most convenient for you and most inconvenient for the opposition. If opposing coaches notice you are doing this expect the same treatment in return and if others are doing it to you rise above it. If you want to truly prove you are the best then you should be prepared to play at any time or day and against the best possible opposition. The problem with always trying to find the worst time for the opposition is that if people can see you are constantly playing at different times on different days then they will know what you are up to as most teams normally have a regular kick off time and day that they play on. As the home manager you can also call the game off claiming the pitch is unplayable or the weather is too bad even if it's not and you are just using it as an excuse because you are missing players. If you get caught out doing this then the league can fine you but some coaches and teams would prefer to pay a fine and get the game rescheduled than to play it and lose.

If you are playing on a pitch which isn't owned by the club then the pitch owners may dictate whether it is playable or not so that decision may be out of your hands even if you wanted to play the fixture. If your club owns the ground then you still have to think long term, it's alright getting one game on in terrible conditions but if it tears up the pitch it may mean that you can't play at home for a month after the game so as a coach you have to take all these things in to consideration when deciding to postpone a game or not. Sometimes it will be a fifty / fifty call - especially if the away team have to travel a long distance. Because of the distance the away team have to travel you will have to give them a fair bit of advance warning so it could be raining heavily at the time the away team were set to leave but by the time they get to the ground the weather could have eased. This means you can get in to situations where you have to make a judgment call and guess what the weather is going to do.

If your game is going ahead then you have to start getting the pitch ready. You will need the nets and corner flags. If you are lucky they may already be set up for you but normally you will have to get them out of a lock up or pick them up from someone's house. This is why the vehicle of choice for a youth football coach should be a van or a people carrier so you can fit all this stuff in. If the match accessories are in a lock up you need to make sure you have the key as normally when you get to a ground and need something everybody you try to call won't answer their phone.

If you are coaching mini soccer then you will need to set up the smaller plastic goals. Some of these goals should need a qualification to set up as they come in a million and one pieces with an IKEA style instruction manual. If you are using mini soccer goals be sure in advance of the game that you know how to set them up and that you have all the pieces with nothing missing

After the corner flags and goals are set up you may need to do extra pitch maintenance; like forking the turf, putting sand down in the goals if they have become too sticky, trying to get rid of mole hills, getting rid of rubbish from the pitch and even repainting the lines if they have disappeared. This is why it is important to know the state of your pitch in advance. If you are trying to do all this before kick-off it will be an absolute nightmare. It will also be up to you to make sure any facilities that you use are unlocked so if you have the keys it will mean unlocking changing rooms and making sure they are tidy, unlocking car park gates or gates to get in to the ground. If you don't possess the keys it is important to let the key holder know before the game that you need things unlocking so they can be ready and waiting on the day.

If you are in a league where the home team have to supply the referee, the week before the game you will have probably spent countless hours on the phone trying to find one. When you do find one make sure you give them all the information and make sure you take their contact details with you to the game and a mobile to call them on in case they don't show up, get lost or are delayed. If you are in a league where the league organises the ref still be sure to get their contact details for the same reasons as again you don't want to be stuck at the pitch with no clue where the ref is as it is your responsibility to make sure they show up!

If you play at a pitch where balls can fly on to a road or down a bank it is useful to try and find ways to stop this from happening or to get someone to be a ball boy for you. If there are any dangers in and around your pitch it is up to you to inform both sets of players and spectators about where they are and what they are. In the case of a medical emergency you also need to know where the nearest hospital is or who the nearest first aider is and where the first aid kit is.

As the home coach you are expected to provide the match ball. It is up to you whether you lay on any refreshments for your visiting team and referee although this isn't mandatory. It will also be up to the home coach to pay any fees and expenses to the referee as directed to by the league.

As the home team coach it is up to you to try and generate the atmosphere you want at your ground. This could mean anything from bringing in a stereo to play music before a game, to holding a raffle. As a coach at the beginning of the season you should inform players and spectators of how they should behave and at a home game you should try and get as many spectators in as possible. If you want to get a big crowd you can advertise the game in the local area and in the local press. When the spectators get to the ground if you want them a certain distance from the pitch you can set up barriers and if you want spectators from your team on the other side to the opposition spectators then again that's your call. It's your pitch so you decide who is allowed on it and how close people are allowed to be.

If trouble breaks out at the ground it is up to you to deal with it. As the home coach you have the power to stop the game and ask people to leave if you feel that their behaviour is inappropriate. You are responsible for people's safety and this should be your number one priority regardless of what the score in the game is. Now most games will go off without any trouble but it's important to be prepared in case anything happens. If you know you have parents or spectators who are a bit volatile you have to be aware of what they are up to and be prepared to ban them from games if you have to.

If this wasn't enough you can't forget your main responsibility which is getting your team warmed up, letting them know the tactics and coaching them throughout the game – this is obviously at the top of your priorities. For home games it's good to have a team of volunteers so they can take some of the stress of setting up away from you so you can focus more on your team.

Being at home should be an advantage for your team so you shouldn't let all your other jobs make it a disadvantage for your team.

Be prepared and learn from each game. If you have a team coming to visit who you have had problems with in the past make sure you do all you can to diffuse the situation. If you think there could be problems get someone from the league or local FA to attend so they can monitor the situation. Saying this, though, a game which you think beforehand may pass off without any trouble may be the worst game of the season for bad behaviour.

If all this wasn't enough after the game as a coach you will then be the last one left clearing things up, taking nets down, taking corner flags in and locking up. A game which lasts under ninety minutes could see you out of the house for three to four hours.

As a coach make your home ground somewhere you are proud to play and where your players are comfortable playing. Your home should be your fortress where you have confidence to play and win matches so you then have a strong base to work off when you go to away matches. You should always be looking at ways in which you can improve your home ground and your home game experience.

Away Games

In youth football it always seems that fixtures are either early Saturday or Sunday morning. If you are an adult coach or parent this means that you either have to forgo a night out on the town or be prepared to wake up extremely tired and with a headache from the night before; not the best combination for attending a youth football match. As a coach you will have told your players at training to get a good nights sleep before the game but it's a case of "do as I say and not as I do", as I daresay you won't have had an early night.

If you are coaching an under 16's team you don't have to worry about whether you go out the night before a game, as it is your players you have to worry about when they start hitting that age where they want to go out on a Friday or Saturday night. If you do go out in the local town the evening before the game it can be a good way of seeing which of your players are out late, especially if you live in a small town.

If you are the type of coach where the team is your life and more important than your job or your family then you wouldn't be out on the town the night before a game. Instead the night before the game you will be stressing about every little tactical decision to make in the game. In your head you will be going through all your players' strengths and weaknesses and if you have played the opposition before you will be trying to remember what they were like when you last played them and what their pitch was like. Then you will be waking up at all hours checking you have got all the equipment, kits and refreshments you need to avoid a last minute panic in the morning.

Like I mentioned in the previous chapter the way away games are set up varies from league to league. In some cases the league will decide on the time and date of a game, but in many leagues it will be up to the home team to decide on the time and day of the fixture with the league only stipulating which weekend the game should be played on. If you are in a league where the home team dictates it can leave you in a tricky situation. Normally your players will have a million and one other things they do or are involved with so when you are the away team, you have to hope the home team picks a day and time which is suitable for your players. It is hard to prepare for a game when the fate of the squad you take to the match rests in the hands of the opposition coach. Of course the coach who has the home game is going to pick a day and time which suits them and their players but it can make your job that much harder. If you are playing a team local to you and the opposition manager knows you have players who are unavailable on certain times and days then they may on purpose select a time and day to be as inconvenient for you as possible. Then based on the players you have out missing you will have to readjust your tactics and formation accordingly which will almost always not be to your benefit.

On the night before the game and the morning of the game you will be waiting by your phone, especially if the weather is bad, to see if the game is still going ahead. If you can't get your first choice squad together you pray for bad weather and at any sign of a slight down pouring you will be ringing the opposition manager trying to persuade them to call the game off. Every other time the phone rings you will be hoping you aren't getting calls from those parents saying they can't drive to the game anymore as their other child has something else on or their car is having problems and all these other last minute emergencies that make your job that bit harder.

On the morning of an away game your main hope is that all your players have remembered the time to meet. When you tell your players information at training it's usually in one ear and out the other so no matter how many times you tell them you always turn up at the meeting place wondering who will remember and who will forget. When going to away games your team will need a meeting place in your town to gather the team before making the journey to the game. When deciding on a meeting time you have to allow time to get to the ground, traffic, getting lost, players turning up late to the meeting place and allow time for a warm up before the game which normally means leaving terribly early - especially if you have never been to the ground you are travelling to before.

As a manager it's up to you to know where you are going to play so parents will come to you expecting you to be their navigator and explain the route - regardless of whether you have been to the pitch before or not! Before the game you will have checked to see how many parents are planning to drive to the game, and how many spare seats they will have to see if you can get all your players there. Normally when it comes time to meet at your meeting place, which in my case was normally a supermarket or leisure centre car park, all your plans will be in disarray as one of the parents will have pulled out or a parent may have decided to bring the entire family so they no longer have those three spare seats. This is why you always have to allow for some extra seats when you are planning lifts to make sure everyone gets there. If you run a team in which very few parents drive, own a car, or have a Driving License it can make getting to away games near on impossible especially in rural areas where there is little or no public transport. Then on top of this, if you run a team in a younger age group because of new laws you have to think about car booster seats and other such fun legalities. So even before you have left your local town you have already encountered a million and one headaches which will take your stress and blood pressure levels up to another level even before a ball has been kicked.

When you finally have everyone ready to leave which will normally be five to fifteen minutes later than when you wanted to leave, you then as a coach have to lead the convoy of cars to the ground. You start out in convoy but by the time you get on the main road you will all be split up as it is impossible to drive in a convoy of five or more cars and then parents will start thinking they know a better route than you so will confuse everyone by turning off in a different direction. Unlike big Premiership grounds, local youth football pitches aren't signposted the only thing you can hope for is that you are playing at a school as that might be signposted. Then to confuse you even more there are teams which don't actually play in the town or village they represent so you end up following signs for a place they don't actually play in.

Driving in a convoy, particularly when you are not sure on where you are going, is very stressful. Especially when you have a car of hyperactive youngsters. All too often you will end up taking a wrong turn, leading everyone down the wrong way or into a dead end which is just a pain in the neck to get out of so when you finally find the ground you are playing at you are just glad to have made it and the game of football is secondary. There is that the odd occasion though, where you think you have found the pitch just to find that the team no longer play there or that someone has directed you to the wrong pitch. This leaves you scrambling for the opposition manager's mobile phone number to find out where the ground is and apologising profusely for being late.

After getting to the ground in a cold sweat you then have to remember about all your tactics for the match and things you want to say to your players which in the state of madness of trying to find the ground would have completely escaped your brain. Then when you have your players on the pitch the home team and referee will want to get on with the game so will only give you ten minutes to get warmed up and ready instead of the thirty minutes you had planned if you weren't late. As you are rushed you don't get chance to say all that you wanted to say to the players or do a proper warm up and the rushed atmosphere descends on your players as no one is one hundred percent ready and prepared for the game as the whistle goes and the game kicks off.

The only saving grace of being the away team is that you don't have to put the nets on the goals up, put the corner flags in, mark out the pitch, provide the match ball or sort out the referee but give me that any day over going to an away game.

In professional football the advantage of playing at home is that most of the fans in the ground are supporting you. In youth football that doesn't always ring true as sometimes you can get more parents that go to away games than go to your home games. Some teams you go and visit will have a large following of parents while others will only have a few and even some where it will just be the coach who is there with no other spectators. The advantage of playing at home in youth football is knowing how to play on your pitch. When you go to away games you don't know how big or small the pitch is going to be, how much of a slant the pitch is going to be on, how big or small the goals are going to be and what the actual state of the turf is like. If you can win a youth league it is truly a testament to being able to play on any surface. FA laws and measurements go out the window when it comes to youth football as if the pitches were inspected I'm sure most wouldn't meet FA standards.

During my time in youth football I have seen it all from molehills on the pitch to playing on a pitch right next to the ocean where in the space of one game five balls were lost in the sea. Even in youth football teams will take whatever advantage they can get so they will adapt their play to suit their pitch and make it hard for the opposition to play on it. Teams will do anything from not cutting the grass to muddying the goal areas; anything they think will give them an advantage. Another thing home teams will do is set themselves up on the side of the pitch they want to start on so I always tell my teams on away games if they win the toss to change sides.

Some teams I have coached have played better away from home and some have found it harder to play away from home. Some times teams find it easier to play away as there can be less parents there and there is less pressure to win away from home. Some young people react better to new environments seeing it as a more important game than a game at their home ground as they play their regularly so are more up for the away game. There is nothing like beating a team in their own back yard. Then you get the flipside of the coin where some teams don't like playing away as they are unsure of new environments so are less confident and go in to their shells. They need to be in their own town in front of their own supporters to feel confident and not in any danger.

As a manager and a parent you have to watch your behaviour even more at away games as you are not on your own patch. In most situations coaches and parents will be more subdued when they go to away games but this isn't always the case and when this isn't the case things can get out of hand.

Regardless of the result; win, draw or loss, after an away game the best thing to do is to get out of there as quickly as possible. Shake hands, pack up and leave. The longer you stay there the more chance there is of getting in to disputes over decisions, tackles and behaviour during the game. When you play a team away for the first time you have to remember that they have to come back to your ground so they should be quite behaved. It's when you have problems during your home games, and when you know you still have to play that team away that going to play them can become quite a nervous experience.

Facilities

In youth football facilities can leave a lot to be desired, with no laws or regulations on what teams have to provide. You can play games anywhere from a farmers field to a local park. There won't be many youth teams that own their own pitches and facilities. Most youth teams will play on a pitch belonging to a Parish council, local council, school or a local men's football team. This means you never know what facilities there are going to be at the pitch you are going to. If they have toilets which are open during the game you think you are playing in the lap of luxury.

Just because the pitch may be a school pitch it doesn't necessarily mean that they will have changing or toilet facilities as the school may not open these facilities for the football. The golden rule is that whenever you are travelling to an away game make sure that your players come to the game ready in their kit underneath their jackets and tracksuits, and to make sure your players go to the toilet before they leave. If you are coaching boys they can at least, if desperate, go up against a hedge but if you are coaching a girls team it can make away games very difficult without toilets or changing facilities. Not only do you have to think of your players but also their parents as well.

As a coach you want as many parents and supporters to turn out for your games as possible but if there are no facilities for them it makes it harder for you to encourage them to come. Then you have rainy days when there is no shelter for them and when the car park is so far from the pitch that they can't see the pitch from their car.

Now I'm not saying all pitches and grounds are this bad. At some grounds, if you are lucky, they will have changing facilities, toilets and even somewhere to purchase food and a hot drink. These are going to become the away games you love. The one small problem with going away to a team with good facilities is when you have to invite them back to your ground you may feel embarrassed by your lack of facilities compared to them.

With the increased need for housing in many villages, towns and cities it means there are less pitches for youth football teams. This means that many sporting clubs are now having to pitch share. Football teams are playing on cricket pitches and rugby teams are playing on football pitches. All of this means even if you are the home team trying to arrange a pitch can be an absolute nightmare. If you use a school pitch you have to be sure to book the pitch you need early as they will normally let many different sporting clubs use their pitches.

If you are using a pitch belonging to a local men's football team trying to arrange dates and times for your games can be difficult. Of course the men's team gets first pick and even if they are playing in the afternoon they won't want anyone else going on before them and damaging the pitch, so when they play at home it rules one day out completely. For facilities, playing at a men's pitch is great as they normally have a shelter and changing rooms but you are completely in their hands and at any minutes notice they can stop you from playing on the pitch if they feel the pitch isn't holding up well which leaves you rushing around trying to find another pitch.

If you have your own pitch it still might be difficult to organise a time as you may have to share the pitch with a number of different age group teams within your organisation. This can cause all sorts of problems as if all the teams are at home on the same day it can mean that you have to get a lot of games on that one pitch and all it takes is for one game to be late to then throw all the other games out of sequence. Another point to remember is that youth football pitches aren't maintained with professional groundsmen like professional clubs, so if a pitch is overused, and if a lot of older aged teams use it then it will get churned up quickly and get to a state where it can't be repaired and is ruined for the remainder of the season.

Because most teams don't own their own pitches it makes it impossible for them to upgrade facilities even if they had the money or wanted to. Then I know of some clubs who have built huts or put in Portacabins only for them to be set on fire or vandalised by local troublemakers. As a football team you are a target of disgruntled ex-players and opposing teams so this is why many teams decide not to have facilities as they don't want to have to deal with these issues and the cost implication involved.

If you suffer from a lack of pitches it can affect what you can do as an organisation as even if you have youngsters that want to play football if you don't have the facilities you can't start extra teams. With a lack of pitches you can also come unstuck if during the season your pitch becomes unplayable, as it may mean that a lot of your teams can't play home fixtures. Some organisations will just start as many teams as possible and then expect local organisations to help them out or use it as a way to pressurise local organisations in to giving them pitches but this isn't a sensible way to run a football club as there is no guarantee you can get those extra young players football matches.

Some organisations will let you use their facilities for free, but most will want to charge you to use their pitches and for the upkeep of the pitch which if you are only using a pitch ten times a year you can't then justify having to pay a weekly or monthly fee all year round for upkeep.

The only way around these problems is to buy your own plot of land from an estate agent or at an auction and turn it in to a pitch. This isn't cheap and finding the right piece of land can take some time. Then when you have the land you have to do all the landscaping and building associated with it. If you have parents of players who are in the building and landscaping trade then it may be affordable to build a ground, but if you don't it can become too expensive. And all of this is even before you have had it health and safety checked and got the insurance you need to run a football ground!

Going to an away game with excellent facilities can make losing a game that bit more bearable. I remember one game as a kid when we lost an away game but we could get a bacon butty from the tea hut so we all went home happy.

Because of the lack of changing facilities at most grounds it means that if you are taking players in your car to games, especially on wet days that there is a good chance that you are going to have to spend some of your time after a game cleaning the mud off of your car seats. That is, of course, if you can get the mud off. For some reason when it's tipping down with rain players love doing dives and sliding tackles which get them absolutely caked in mud.

If you are going to an away ground another issue will often be parking. If you are playing at a school or near a leisure centre there is normally parking but with some council, park and parish pitches there may be no parking which means you have to park beside a busy road or a mile away from the pitch itself. Then you have some pitches where you have to park on the grass alongside the pitch. This means that during the game it is more than likely that each car will get hit with a ball at some point and that when it comes time to leave if it has been raining you may need a four wheel drive vehicle to get you out as the cars begin to get stuck in the mud. Sometimes schools can also be frustrating for parking as they can lock up a lot of its facilities over the weekend so parking isn't a guarantee, and the way schools are designed these days sometimes makes it impossible to work out which way is the main entrance and which entrance is the nearest to the football pitches.

Sometimes it is nice to go to a ground where there are a lot of pitches and games happening at the same time as it creates a bit of a carnival atmosphere. However this does mean that finding the pitch you're supposed to be playing on can be a nightmare and that all the teams are sharing a couple of changing rooms. For a coach it also creates havoc as there are whistles going off everywhere and trying to communicate with your players can be a waste of time as they can't hear you above the noise.

So with facilities always expect the worst. Most regular football goers will go with a boot filled with everything they may need from a tow rope to bin liners to cover the seats with or to sit down on and watch the game. In youth football you have to be prepared for everything and bring anything with you that can keep you warm, clean or get you out of the ground as it will make going to the game just that bit more enjoyable.

Referees

Without Referees there wouldn't be youth football. Plain and simple. Not many people want to be, or have the character, to be a football referee. Unlike in the Premiership where there are barriers and stewards between the referee and the angry supporters, cameras that film every moment and players that have to try and be role models, none of this exists in local youth football. On some occasions the referee of a local youth football match can be more worried about getting out of the ground safely than about their performance.

When you have forty thousand fans in a Premiership stadium shouting abuse at the referee it's just noise and it is hard for the referee to pick out individual faces of the abusers. In local youth football it is easy to see who the people shouting abuse are as there won't be many people there so it is more personal. The referee in local youth football will then have to walk past the same spectators that may have been abusing them to leave the pitch, and go to the same car park to get their car to leave the ground with no one stopping the angry spectators from coming up and speaking their mind.

In local men's football it's the players which are going to cause the referee the most grief and problems, whereas in youth football more often than not it is the parents who are the problem. If a parent sees a referee not disciplining a player that has fouled their child, or giving a free kick against their child then the referee will become public enemy number one and normally a tirade of abuse will follow. If the parent is a 'win-at-all-costs' type of parent then they will complain at any perceived injustice to the team as a whole and not just their own child.

Just like the players and spectators in local youth football the facilities for referees will be limited with no safe place to store your things whilst you are out on the pitch and no shelter to be had at half time. If you are very lucky one of the clubs may offer you a drink or an orange at half time but teams who do this will be few and far between. You will take abuse for the length of the game and then you will be asked if you can do the next game and come back to do it all over again.

In local youth football some referees will claim expenses or receive a fee that the league sets for how much you have to pay the referee. This is usually a nominal amount which may just cover expenses. Many referees however will waive the fee as if a club has, say, ten home games a season and the fee for a ref is ten pounds per game then that means it is an extra one hundred pounds that the team has to find a season and if there are a number of age groups at the club the bill can really start to rack up.

As a youth football coach finding a referee can be an art form. Each year your local league or FA will issue you with a handbook which has the names and phone numbers of all the referees in your area. It will then be the responsibility of the home manager to find a referee. Some leagues will appoint referees to games for you which makes life much simpler, but if you are in a league where you have to find a referee hours of your week and pounds on your phone bill can be spent trying to find one for your matches. As a coach you will go down the list hearing every excuse under the sun as to why a ref can't do a game. You will leave countless answer phone messages and find out that twenty of the refs on the list have either quit or the details listed for them are no longer correct. This is why, as a coach, when you find a referee that will do one game for you it's important to try and look after them and get them to do all your home games. Having the same ref for every game may not be an ideal situation but it beats spending hours of your week on the phone trying to secure a referee, freeing up more time to focus on other areas. If the referee does all your games it can become a situation where you are too friendly with the ref and know each other on first name terms, breeding ill feeling with the opposition. If you are on first name terms with the ref the opposition may think the referee is awarding you decisions because you are friends with them. In some cases if a decision goes against the home team which the coach of the home team didn't agree with then a rift can develop between the home manager and the referee as they may expect the referee to favour their team.

If you can't find a qualified referee then you have to find someone who has some basic knowledge of the game to act as your referee. Nine times out of ten this will be a parent or a relative of one of your players. Youth football will be one of the only places where you will find situations where someone related to a player or team will referee, again not the best way to run a football match but as a coach you will normally just want to get games played so would accept anyone refereeing it. If you are a relative refereeing a game it puts you in an awkward position as if you give a decision against the home team then your friends and parents of players will give you a hard time. You won't be able to live a wrong decision down, or if you give a decision against the away team and they know you are a relative of a player on the home team, you will be accused of being biased. If the away team know the ref is related to the home team they may also put in a complaint with the league about it if they are unhappy with the performance. The league you are in will stipulate who can and who can't referee your games. Some will stipulate that the referee must be qualified where some will let anybody do it.

Sometimes even worse than a parent refereeing can be another coach of a different age group within the club especially when they turn up to referee the game in the club tracksuit which immediately will get the back up of the opposition. Even if the other coach comes along without the tracksuit, in local youth football circles most clubs have teams in various age groups so everyone knows each other and most people will recognise your ref as a coach of another age group. Even worse than all of this is when the coach of the team that is playing referees the game. When as an away team you have travelled miles to get to a game and the coach of the home team says they will referee it as they have no one else to do it you will probably still play the game as you have travelled all that distance even though it is usually against the rules and that you are not happy about it. I feel sympathy for coaches who get no support and it is just them trying to do it all with no help from anyone else but the rules are the rules and it puts you in an awkward position. Now the games I have been to when coaches have refereed them have always gone fine but there will always be that one case when you will wish you had never agreed to play the game.

When the game is in play no matter what you think of the referee and decisions they are giving it is up to you to lead by example and not to complain about the ref no matter how biased or bad you may think they are. It is also up to you to make sure that your players are playing to the whistle and not answering back to the ref whilst at the same time you need to make sure your parents are not abusing the ref. This is of course if you are doing what you should be doing as a coach. Some coaches won't do this and these are the ones that normally fall in to the win-at-all-costs category. These coaches will normally either do one of two things. They will either try and be over friendly with the ref to try and persuade them to give decisions for their team or they will do what is commonplace and put the referee under so much pressure over every decision that the ref gives the decision to their team as they know the abuse they will get if they don't give it. The way the coach behaves will dictate how their players and parents act towards the referee so when you have all the players, parents and coaches questioning the referee's every decision it can turn youth football in to a very stressful environment when it is suppose to be something people do for fun and enjoyment.

As a coach your players will watch football on TV and react to the referee the way they see their idols doing it on TV. If their favourite player mouths off to the referee and is always in their face then that is how they are going to behave on the pitch as they just want to be like their idol. As a coach if you see coaches on the TV giving the referee abuse then again you may think it is acceptable for you to do it, so I blame a lot of the way we behave towards referees on what we see on TV.

A referee for many is just a punching bag for them to get out their aggression and stress built up during the week. Instead of shouting at their children, other half, friends or work colleagues they will store it all up and let it go on the referee every weekend.

It's not just the referee who will be on the end of abuse from players and spectators as the assistant referees will also get their share. In youth football assistant referees are usually what used to be known as club linesmen. This is when each team is asked to provide someone to fulfil assistant referee duties. This is where most spectators try and hide or come up with some excuse why they can't do it. The person chosen normally has no qualifications to do it but has been to many football games. It is then their job to take a flag and give decisions for throw-ins and offsides, it is up to the referee to manage them, make sure they are doing their job and not cheating. For some reason most coaches will think that the assistant ref is in charge of throw ins and offside decisions but actually it is the referee who is in charge of those decisions and the assistant referee is only giving their opinion on what it should be which the referee can go with or overrule at any time. However if the referee overrules an assistant referee the coach will give them grief and say things like "it was offside" if the assistant ref had his flag up even if the coach is nowhere near being in line with the offside so has no clue whether it was on or offside. Coaches somehow have the ability to be able to see everything that is happening on the pitch from wherever they stand, which will include them having x-ray vision to be able to see through players for incidents happening on the far side of the pitch.

In my time in football I have seen club linesmen do all sorts of things whilst running the line including walking the dog, chatting on the phone, eating a Cornish Pasty and trying to light a cigarette; and people say men can't multi-task! After the game club linesmen will have a go at the ref if they do overrule them or don't go with their decisions because they don't know that it is up to the ref to make the decisions. If you are lucky enough to get qualified and appointed assistant refs to games it can make life much easier but still then some coaches will continue to give them abuse.

If a coach doesn't have any support from the parents of the players then sometimes the coach will be the assistant referee which again isn't right, and is against most league rules. Normally when a coach runs the line they are so engrossed in coaching their team that they aren't paying attention to the game and getting the decisions right. When you are refereeing or running the line you shouldn't be coaching your players which most people are able to do but some just can't help themselves and end up spending most of the game coaching instead of doing what they should be doing. If you are coaching whilst refereeing or running the line it will normally bring you a complaint or abuse from the opposing coach and spectators.

So if you don't want to spend hours every week trying to find a referee, treat referees with respect. If you are in a league which arranges referees for you it's still important that you respect your referee. If you get a reputation for harassing refs then none of the referees will want to officiate your games so again you may end up without a referee. If we don't look after referees it's only going to mean more refs leaving the game which will mean more cancelled games every week. The numbers of referees are thin enough as it is without us forcing more referees out of the game. Like coaches enjoy coaching refs want to go out and enjoy refereeing without the hassle that comes with it.

Opposing Managers

In your league you will come up against a wide range of opposing managers. Some that will be doing it just to give kids a game every week, some that are in it to win everything, some that want to coach good football, some that just want something to take their aggression out on and some that are doing it because nobody else would and want to keep the club going.

Some opposing managers you will get on with and some you won't, just like being back at school. Normally coaches will be nice as pie to each other in the run up to the game and before the game but during the game and after the game it's another story. In some games instead of the game being about the children and the competition between two sets of players, the game turns into a war between the two coaches.

You will get two main breeds of coach. The first one being the coach that likes to get all the accolades for being a great coach and wants all the headlines. The second one is the coach that wants to be a good coach but lets their players get all the credit and is happy to hide away in the background. Coaching is not something you can be in for yourself, it's not about you winning or getting respect. It's about developing your players and making them the best they can be whilst still enjoying playing the game of football.

Some coaches like to wind each other up and if a coach can see that they can easily wind another coach up they will. Sometimes rivalry between teams can be just down to the coaches not the players on the pitch. There are some coaches that other coaches would like to get the upper hand on. Some coaches who have successful teams will be smug and get under the skin of other coaches and coaches will always have rival coaches they don't want to lose to.

You can never trust what another coach tells you. Cynical I know but it's true. A coach may tell you that they are struggling for numbers or their best players are out before the game but when you get there all of their best players are playing, it happens in the Premiership so I'm not surprised it happens in youth football. If their team loses some coaches will not admit the best team won instead they will say their team played the worst they had ever played or come up with some excuse for the loss blaming the ref, the weather or claiming players weren't fully fit, saying anything not to accept that they were beaten fairly and squarely.

Then there are coaches who will cheat to win. Yes this does happen in youth football. Some coaches will illegally register players who are unable to play in the league due to being registered to other clubs or being the wrong age to play. This will involve anything from giving them a different name, someone else's photo or doctoring their date of birth on a Birth Certificate. If they can't get them registered they may play them and just put down a different name for them. They will deliberately get someone to referee for them who isn't qualified and who they know will be biased towards their team. Anything you can think of, they will try it.

If they aren't breaking the rules they are bending them. If they haven't got all their players for a game they will call the game off after only a spot of rain, or they will claim that they have all come down with flu even if it is the middle of the summer. They see every game as so important that they cannot afford to lose a game and don't think they can win without their so-called star players.

When calling a game off an opposing manager may wait until the last second possible to do it just to wind the opposing manager up. They may try and change venues, times, days - anything just to annoy them. If they think they can get an upper hand by getting under your skin they will.

Some coaches will be that notorious that when you get together with other coaches in the league you will spend your time talking about the coaches you don't get on with and most of the other coaches in your league will know who the notorious coaches are. This is what makes the games where you get on with the opposition coach and when they go out of their way for you and your team more enjoyable. Some coaches will use common sense and will want both teams to be able to play their best teams so even if they have the right to choose when kick off is will arrange a day and time that suits you as well as them and are willing to accommodate you. Away games are always much better when the home coach comes and greets you and makes you feel welcome at the ground which is commonplace but as a coach you don't expect it everywhere you go.

If you try and get on with your opposing coaches it will make your life much easier and the way to deal with coaches you don't get on with is to not rise to them and just continue to let your team's football do the talking.

Parents

As a youth team coach the parents of your players will become your supporters, your critics, your helpers, and your advisers that you never asked for. As a coach you need your parents as without them you wouldn't be able to get your players to games and training sessions. At some point in the season you are going to have to rely on a parent for something so as a coach you need to keep them on your side.

You want as many parents to come to games and support their children as possible. However you are not always going to get all the parents there as some see football like a childminding service where they can drop their child off for a couple of hours and come back and collect them afterwards. Other parents will work on the weekends meaning they can't get to games. As a coach there is nothing more disheartening than when you are at a home game and the away support outnumbers yours so as a coach you should be doing all you can to encourage parents to come and watch their children.

Different parents will put in different levels of activity in to the club. Some parents only want to come and cheer on their child, some parents will volunteer to help out washing kit and help you set out the pitch for home games, some parents will help with lifts, some parents will volunteer to raise money and some parents will want to be your chief tactical adviser.

As a coach many people will think they can do a better job than you are doing regardless of whether you are winning or losing. Parents will come up with all kinds of suggestions to where you should play players, what formation you should use and what you should be doing in training. Normally this advice will come during a game from all corners distracting you from doing your job. The problem with the advice is that everyone has a different opinion and all these people offering opinions aren't coaches. Watching Match of the Day is sometimes the closest some have come to football. One thing I have noticed in my years of youth football is that it's normally those parents that are unwilling to help out and who just come to watch their child who are offering this advice and you know full well that they aren't going to back it up with offers of help. If you don't follow their advice and go on to lose a game they will let you know about it, citing that if you had followed their advice you would have won.

The problem with the advice is even if it is sound advice, if you are seen taking advice from a parent then everyone else will want to throw their two pennies worth in and you will forever be managing by committee, constantly having your ear bent by all and sundry when all you want to do is focus on a training session or a match. If you do listen to their advice and then don't use it then you are in an even worse position than not listening in the first place. If you are winning but not following advice then there won't be that much of a backlash, but if you are losing and not taking advice then parents can get on your back but in this situation you need to be a strong manager and stick to your guns. At the end of the day if the team loses it falls on your shoulders and not those of the parents.

Some parents will want their children to be strikers. These parents want their children to be the one grabbing the glory and scoring goals every weekend. However if you had ten strikers and nobody in defence or midfield you would lose every game. As soon as you cave to one parent's request then all the other players and parents will want to do the same and then refuse to play where you put them as they will want to play up front as well. If you put a player up front who isn't a goal scorer and they start missing chances and not scoring it can affect their confidence and have an adverse effect on their enthusiasm but some parents don't think like that. To keep the harmony of the club regardless of how good you think it would be to move a player, and even if you were already planning to do it, if you are seen to be bowing to parent pressure then it won't be long before nobody wants to play in their given position any more.

If results aren't going your way and parents are not getting what they want from you some will either threaten to or actually take their child out of the team. Normally the parent will have already done their research and contacted one of your rivals before threatening that they are going to take their child to play for them to try and pressurise you even more. If the parent knows that their child is one of the better players in the team then they will try and use it to their advantage as they know that you won't want to lose them. Regardless of how good or important a player is you have to treat everyone as equals. You can't give players special treatment and you can't be held to ransom no matter how much you want or need to keep a player. If a parent has done this once to get their own way there is nothing to say that they won't try this stunt again. Letting a good player get what they or their parent wants will send a bad message to your team and can have a damaging result on morale. If this does happen and you pander to the parents and the children you may start losing other players from the team so you are just causing yourself more long-term problems.

Some parents will start helping out and be the first one to volunteer to help so they can get in your ear. They will start off by just helping you and won't mention anything about football but as the weeks develop they will try to form a close bond with you, then start giving you advice or pointers. In some clubs many parents will play the game of 'who can get closest to the coach' and 'who can get their opinions heard'. Parents want to be in control of situations that their child is in and football is no different. Now many parents will volunteer just because they want to help out but you always have to be wary.

Some parents will try anything to get close to a coach like invite them round for meals, volunteer to drive them to games, buy them presents and even get them jobs. The one thing to remember even in youth football is there is no such thing as a free meal and if you start taking gifts and handouts then you have be prepared that the parent will expect to have their voice heard. As a coach you either want to drive to away games yourself or get a lift with another coach as if you get a lift with a parent they may see it as their chance to discuss everything they think that you need to do and if it is a long trip you will end up with earache especially on the way home if you end up losing the game and not following their advice.

A big problem you can encounter with parents is that if you start their child as a substitute, substitute their child during the game, or have their child as a substitute and never bring them on. For some reason many parents would prefer you to play their child in the wrong position rather than them being a substitute. For some reason there is a stigma around being a substitute that you are somehow not as good as the players on the pitch. Parents will also remember how many times their child has been a substitute compared to all the other players and how much game time they have got compared to everyone else. If they see their child being a substitute a lot they may come to you as a coach and ask for reassurances that their child will start the next match.

If a parent has had to travel to an away game and their child doesn't get played then you as a coach will be public enemy number one. If there is one thing parents don't like, it's travelling for no reason. So as a coach be sure to make sure all your subs get on the pitch if you don't want earache from the parents.

One thing to remember is to always pick your team based on the effort they give in training and their talent. Don't play players just because you know if you pick them their parents will drive to an away game for you as that is not fair on the players. On the other side don't ask parents of players to do you favours if you know that their child may not get much time on the field as the parents will think you are using them.

As a coach the key things to do are to show you appreciate the parents of your players and to take an interest in their lives but whenever they offer you advice the best thing to do is to turn the conversation away from football as quickly as possible. Don't make yourself too accessible, parents have to be comfortable with you as a coach and know how to get hold of you but don't put yourself in a position where you are on the phone to your player's parents most nights and spending too much time before and after training talking to them. The longer you spend speaking with them the more advice they will try to give you.

The problem with getting too close with a parent is that it may cloud your judgement if you are friends with them off the field, or it may make your decision that much harder on who to play. You may take the easy option and pick their child just to keep friends. If you build up a friendship with the parent and then don't play their child it could start world war three so I like to avoid that situation where I can. I think the best thing is to be friendly with your parents as a group but not to spend too much time individually with parents as then other parents may say you are only picking a certain player because you are friends with their mother or father which is not right.

A good idea is to hold a parents meeting at the start of the season so you can set out your stall and let the parents know what to expect, what you will tolerate, and what you won't tolerate. By doing this you are being upfront and honest so that everyone knows where they stand. It's a good idea after every game to thank the parents that have come and show your appreciation. If you can get parents onside, get them supporting the club, and not trying to have a say in tactics then it makes your job much easier.

As a coach it is your job to be responsible for your players parents' behaviour at games. Some parents can get over enthusiastic and carried away at football games. For an hour or more they just forget about everything else that is going on and get caught up in the game, or they will bring all their problems with them that they have had during the week and take their anger out at the football match. Parents will shout at the official if they disagree with a decision, an opposition player if they think they are playing dirty, or the opposition spectators if they disagree with them. When some parents go to a football match all normal behaviour can go out of the window as they become a different person. In my time in youth football I have seen it all from obscenities being traded across the pitch, to heated confrontations, to fights breaking out in the crowd. The parents are supposed to set an example to the children but normally the children are better behaved than the parents and are embarrassed by what is happening around them.

If you witness something going on with your parents you have to divert your attention from the game and sort out the problem, no matter if the parent is ten times your size or a group scuffle has broken out - it is up to you to calm it down. You have to go in, play peacemaker, and calm everyone down. Depending on who owns the land you are playing on and what the referee wants to do you may have to help remove somebody from the ground - especially if you are the home team.

Now these are extreme circumstances and rarely happen but you have to be prepared for them. It is just a shame when you have a good player who has a parent who you can't let go to football matches because of their behaviour. Even if the parent takes the child out because of this you can't tolerate a misbehaving parent so you end up having to lose the player although you hope the parent would let the child continue to come to football even if the club has stopped them from going.

It is hard to predict which matches are going to take place where something may flare up. Sometimes it's the matches you least expect to cause you trouble that end up in chaos so always be prepared for anything when you go to a football match.

Parents have to stump up a lot of money to keep their children involved in football so don't take them for granted. They will pay yearly fees to the club, they will donate money, they will make sure their child is fully kitted out and they will drive to away games which over the season will add up to a bit in petrol money, none of which they can claim back. Without the parents support we wouldn't have youth football so as coaches you need to be appreciative of them.

Stars in their Eyes

Many young footballers dream of being able to play for their favourite team. When they play football they will try and emulate their favourite players, copying moves, skills and mannerisms they have seen on TV. Their bedrooms will be adorned with all the latest club merchandise and they won't be seen out without the shirt of their favourite team on with the name and number of their favourite player on the back.

Instead of playing for the team, players with stars in their eyes will play for themselves and only worry about how good they look. They aren't interested in the result as long as they can score some goals or put in a good performance. These players will want their egos stroked and people to praise them by giving them man of the match awards, captaincy and have people singing their praises.

Unfortunately the sad reality of football is that only a very tiny percentage of children who play football will go on to make a living as a professional footballer. However, due to the way footballers are perceived with the media attention they get, the money they get paid, the lifestyles they lead and the fame they receive it makes youngsters want it even more regardless of how small the odds are. Young people have more belief than adults and regardless of how many times you tell them how hard it is going to be they won't comprehend it. So whatever you say, you won't deter them from their dreams which in a way is a good thing as young people need to be allowed to dream because if they are prepared to work hard enough they can achieve their dreams.

Players with stars in their eyes will usually play for more than one team and will only stay with a team if they are winning. As soon as they start losing they will not turn up for training and show a disinterest in the club, paying more interest in their other teams. If you let them, some players will refuse to turn up to training but expect to play in every game as they think they are untouchable, acting as though you need them more than they need you. Players like this will always try and threaten you as a coach telling you that they are going to go to another club or speak openly and outwardly about how rubbish they think the team is, showing no respect for you as a coach. They will think that they are the reason the club performs so well and think it has nothing to do with the coach their training and their tactics.

If a player thinks they are better than the team they will normally disrupt training by questioning every exercise or drill you give them, in some cases even refusing to join in, and if they do participate they won't do it properly. Other players in the team will see this, then they will start acting up and before you know it you have a full on mutiny on your hands. If the other players in the team recognise one player as the best they will look up to them and copy whatever they do.

If you are a coach and you have a player like this it will make your job that much harder. If you try and start them on the bench to bring them back to earth they will normally pull a tantrum or refuse to play. If you put them in a different position than what they want to play, again they will get in a huff but unlike being on the bench they will probably play but not listen to a word you say and play in the position they want to play when they get out on to the field. To make things even worse if you try and sub them off they may refuse to come off the pitch which puts you as a coach in a terrible situation as the game will be held up when everybody else wants to get on with the game and you are trying to convince a player to come off. If a player is perceived as better than everyone else you will have to deal with flack from all sides if you put them on the bench as then other players will start moaning saying that they can't win without them, with even some of the parents questioning your decisions so it turns into a no-win situation. Taking off your best players or not selecting them sends a clear signal to everyone; to your players, parents, and opposition that all is not well in your club and it may look to the outside world that you are having problems controlling your team. People will wonder about your coaching skills, even though you are doing the right thing and trying to instil some discipline in your team. Some may think that you are putting politics and petty squabbles ahead of picking the best team which people presume you should always do every week regardless of what is going on.

Sometimes it won't be the media that are putting stars in the eyes of young players, sometimes it will be their parents. A parent is always going to think their child is the best and want the best for them regardless of what skill level their child is at. In youth football parents can be the equivalent of agents in the professional game. Some parents will tout their children to clubs looking for the best offer for their child to play, and looking for the best team for their child to play in. They will not be interested in the success of the club their child is playing in and will only be interested in the success of their own child.

Parents like this will be the first to let the coach know if they don't think their child is getting the right training or isn't being played in the right position on match days. These parents will show commitment as they will attend every training session and match day but normally the reason for this is so that they can get in to the coaches ear, putting them under pressure and keep a close eye on their child's development.

These parents will be willing to turn their own lives upside down to support their child. They will take time off from work, give up their free time and spend every last penny they have on kit, equipment, travelling and coaching for their child. They will cart their child off to every trial and training session they find out about regardless of where in the country it is. Normally the parent will have an idea on what professional club they want their child to end up at so they will try and get their child in to any youth football team, trials or training that the professional club hold. In amongst all the carting around they will be in touch with scouts trying to convince them to come and watch their child play or trying to get their child in to games where a scout will be watching.

When deciding on what club to send their child to, a parent with stars in their eyes will not list things like locality and which team their child's friends play for as top priorities in what they look for. Instead it will be the quality of players they will be playing with, what league the team is in and what connections the coaching staff have with professional clubs. These parents will always be willing to take their child out of a club as soon as a better offer comes along. If they can't get their child in to the team they want them to be in they may even try and convince the players from that team they wanted their child to play in to come and play in the same team as their child. They will do anything to make sure their child is playing in the best team.

If it isn't against a contract that their child has signed the parent with stars in their eyes will want their child to play in as many teams as possible including school teams and as many youth sides as possible. When they haven't got organised training or a game the parent will practice with their child for hours every night regardless of whether the child wants to do it or is it fit enough to do it. If they don't feel like they can coach them to the standard they want they won't be above enlisting or paying a professional coach to help them out. These parents don't think long term of any physical damage they may be doing to their child by over-playing and over-training they will only think of the long term gain. They will try and free up as much of the child's time as possible, stopping them from going out with friends or getting involved in other activities and woe betide them if they want to have girlfriends or boyfriends as they will just be seen as an unneeded distraction. Sometimes morals will go out of the window with a parent with stars in their eyes as they won't see anything wrong with doing their child's homework for them if it means they can spend more hours on football - or if a doctor says their child is injured and can't play they may go to another doctor for a second opinion.

Sabotage can be another trick up the sleeve of a parent with stars in their eyes. They will withhold any contacts or information about trials they have from other players and parents. When it comes to football games they may tell their child not to pass to certain players or to try and make other players look as bad as possible. When someone is obsessed with a professional contract all rules of fair play go out the window.

Some children will be pushed in to football by their parents even if it is not what they want to do, but the child will do it to keep their parents happy. Parents who have a reputation in the community for having been good at football will want someone to continue the family name, somebody they can say they helped to the top. Then you have parents that always wanted to play football at the top level when they were younger who try and live out their dreams through their child or just assume that their child has the same dreams that they did when they were a child. These parents will stop at nothing to see their child reach the top and will keep on pushing them no matter how many knock-backs they have or no matter how slim the chances become of them making it.

Now there are many reasons why a parent may act in this way. Some parents do it for money. They see their child as a way to make money because a professional contract in the Premiership could be worth megabucks and they think their child will pass some of their earnings back to their parents. Their child becomes an investment for them which they are willing to keep investing in for the hope that one day it will get paid back ten fold. If a family lives in a poor situation then they may see a professional contract as the only way out of their situation.

Some parents want the fame and notoriety which comes from being the parent of a professional footballer. They want to be seen as a success, they want the family name to be up in lights. They want all the side perks that come with it like being interviewed by the media and being given freebies from local businesses but more importantly they want people to recognise them when they go out. They want to be stopped in the street to be asked about their child and have people come up to them to ask for their child's autograph. Having a professional footballer for a child can put you in to a higher class, can bring you respect and a new circle of friends.

The problem with parents with stars in their eyes is when it all comes crashing down. When you invest so much time and effort in a dream that doesn't happen it can be soul destroying. It can leave them in financial crisis and leave their child in a predicament of what to do with their life as after investing so much time in football they haven't taken time to look at other career options. The Premiership is a dream factory and in reality only a few dreams can come true.

The financial and career problems may not be the worst after effect of not achieving a professional contract. It can be the damage it does to the child and the family that can be the worst of all. If it was the child's dream to play in the Premiership then having that dream killed will take some recovering from and may affect their confidence in everything else they do. If getting to the Premiership wasn't the child's dream but the parents dream the child may resent their parents for forcing them to dedicate so much of their life to football, and will feel as if they have missed out on a lot of happy memories and time spent as a kid being a kid. In some extreme cases parents may blame their child for the bad financial or family situation they may be in either saying that if it hadn't been for them they wouldn't have invested all the money, or blaming their child for not being good enough to make it. The child may blame themselves for the situation their family finds themselves in from which they may never recover from.

I think as a child and as a parent the key thing to remember is that young people should be able to enjoy playing football. If it's a child's dream to be a professional footballer then the parents should help guide them but never make the child do something they don't want to do. By all means have that aim but don't make a football contract what life is about; always make sure the child has a balanced life and other options in case it doesn't work out. If a child enjoys their youth and becomes a professional footballer then they will always have a happy life to look back on but if a child becomes a professional footballer with a terrible upbringing then later in life the child may think that the sacrifices weren't worth it. If a child is pushed too hard by their family they may have emotional and relationship problems with their family which stops them from enjoying their professional career to the full, and if they can't do that it hasn't been worth it.

Winning at all Costs

If you watch football on TV you will have heard the phrase "It's a results business!" probably more times than you have had hot dinners. The problem with them saying this all the time about football on TV is it breeds that atmosphere and approach to youth football. Yes, in the Premiership there is a lot of money riding on where a team finishes in the league and the cups so it is a results business. Youth football shouldn't be like that and this is where I think this country is going wrong. If we as a country want to develop better players we have to give them the chance to learn, develop and play good football.

Not just play football which wins football matches, forgetting about playing with style, forgetting about playing just basic good football. Nobody learns from playing football which is focused on lumping the ball up the field at every chance you get.

For some children, parents, and coaches winning in youth football can become everything. The whole week before the game they will be thinking of what they need to do to win and then their whole weekend is centred around the match with their mood for the week after being decided by whether they win or lose. The pressure some coaches and parents put teams under to win games is phenomenal; instead of going to enjoy a football game they are going to a game to win with their long term goal to win the league or cup they are in. In the build up to the game there will be no talk of enjoying yourself and doing your best, it will all be about winning and nothing else.

If you are involved in a club like this and your team loses a game then post match talks from the coach can be brutal. Not only are the players down because they lost, they feel they have let the parents and the coach down. This is all compounded when a coach will go off on one ripping into everything the team did wrong instead of praising what they did right. This talk will normally end with the coach saying that if they want to win the league they better play a lot better than they did today.

Some parents and coaches will offer incentives to their players to win with that being anything from a McDonalds to a five pound note. In professional football I agree with bonus incentives for performance but when kids need to be bribed in order to play their best or to have their good play rewarded by cash or a free meal it shows the game is in a sad state of affairs. Kids should just be able to go out, try their best, and enjoy playing football without all these rewards. If they can't just enjoy playing football without having to be rewarded then they are in the wrong sport. As a coach I always hated coaching against teams that offered rewards, because if your players got wind of it they would be asking you if they could have the same things that the opposition get. Yes by all means treat your team from time to time but don't make it the norm as if you are doing it every week it isn't special any more and the players will remember those treats even more if they don't get them every week.

The ugly side of winning at all costs is when coaches ask their players to go out and intentionally foul or hurt a member of the opposition. Stone Age thinking, I know, but I am sure it still happens up and down the country.

When someone's health and wellbeing is risked for a game of football then things have gone too far, and the people who tell players to do that should be kicked out of the football. It's a repetition of the culture where winning is everything and where no one wants to be seen to lose that breeds this stupid thinking. Each player is someone's son or daughter and I'm sure the people telling their players to hurt a member of the opposition wouldn't want it done to their child. Instead of trying to find a way to deal with and counteract good players, the opposition coaches try to take the easy way out by getting them injured as they don't know how to coach against them. If you are brilliant at a sport it shouldn't mean you become a target for other teams to foul or injure you out of the game. Where is the pride and honour of winning by taking someone out?

This then moves us on to the blame culture. When you think you are the best team and want to win every game when it isn't going your way, you will start blaming everyone else for why you are losing. It can't be that the other team is better than your team. Normally it's the referee that will get the brunt of this frustration as every decision they make is questioned. As the game gets closer to the end the more vocal parents and coaches will get to the referee calling them every name under the sun and behaving in a manner towards them which they wouldn't do in the street. People like this see nothing wrong in disrespecting the referee or threatening them. To them, it beats having to admit that their team wasn't good enough on that day and that the other team deserved to win.

A lot of coaches will have a must win attitude but they will be very subtle about it. If a coach is a win at all costs coach they will pander to their so-called better players by letting them get away with behaviour which they wouldn't allow others to get away with. They will pick them regardless of their attitude, if they are a team player, or if they have been to training. Instead of making a stand they will let them play as they see winning the game more important than discipline. If they are missing their best players for a game they will find a way to have the game called off and they may deliberately set a kick off time which means some of the opposition players can't make it.

Then you get the less subtle coach who will build their training sessions and tactics around getting any advantage including cheating to win. They will encourage their players to time waste, to commit fouls out of the view of the referee, to wind up players in the opposition and any other bits of gamesmanship they can think of to help get the result they want. During the game they will shout things at the referee and opposition players to put them under pressure.

The coaches that normally undertake these tactics don't have enough faith and confidence in the ability of their team to win the match they are playing in. They are unwilling to let the game be decided by who is the best team on that given day. As a player, if your own coach doesn't have confidence in you and your team mates who else is going to?

Everyone who plays sport likes to win and young people need to be taught how to compete in a competitive environment as that is what lies ahead for them in adult life, so I am all for football being a competitive sport with results written down and a league table being formed. The younger someone can learn how to deal with defeat and to enjoy success the better as these are valuable skills for them to learn. It's not the result that matters however, it's how your players deal with that result. For long term development, players and teams need to be encouraged to improve and play good football. The governing bodies need to do more to reward and recognise clubs which aren't about winning or losing but are about developing great footballers as that should be your aim as a football club. Wins and losses will be forgotten about over time but as a player you will always know how good you really are. If you ask most young people they just enjoy playing football and forget about the result soon after the game when it is the parents and the coaches who are left worrying about and getting frustrated by a result. Most young people go in to football to make friends and to have a good time - not to win whatever the local league is in your area. As a culture there needs to be less of a stigma about losing and coaches need to put less pressure on their team to win. These young people will have a lot of time when they are older to deal with pressurised situations but when they are young they should be able to play football and enjoy it without wondering what the repercussions will be if they lose – typically in this country a training session of just running or some archaic punishment.

Assistant Coaches

As a coach it is up to you whether or not you get the services of an assistant. Some coaches couldn't work without one and to some they just get in the way but in youth football I personally find an assistant coach is well worth their weight in gold if you can find the right person for the job.

When getting an assistant you have to make sure they are right for the team and that they will be committed. Just because someone was a good player it won't make them a good coach, and just because someone is good with children it won't make them a good coach either.

In an assistant coach you have to make sure you find someone who can take orders and who won't overrule you or undermine you. An assistant coach has to be able to provide feedback and ideas when asked for so they have to know about football and coaching as you want to be able to tap in to their ideas and get the most out of them.

When selling an assistant coaching position to someone you have to stress the importance of the role. Just because it is an assistant position it doesn't mean you want someone that is there only half the time and never contactable. They have to be reliable because if anything happens to you, you have to be able to have faith in them to stand in and to know that they will do the job.

You have to be able to work well with your assistant coach and get on with them on a personal level as when dealing with your team you have to be able to show a united front. If there are any tensions between you the players will be able to spot it right away. You have to both go in with the same philosophy because if your assistant coach is telling a player something different than you did when they asked you a question the player is going to get confused or even worse play off the fact that they can get one of you to say yes to something.

You and your assistant form a team. You both need to know what you expect from each other and what your responsibilities are. As time in training is so short and because game days can be chaotic you both need to know what each other are going to be doing so you know that everything gets done.

Try and keep your assistant coach as involved as possible and make them feel important. Don't just have them doing all the jobs you don't want to do. If you want to keep an assistant coach you have got to give them chance to do some coaching and have an input not just setting up equipment and doing all the admin and behind-the-scenes stuff for the team. If you just give them the worst jobs they may leave and you will be without an assistant coach again. This will probably have an effect on your team and disrupt them. Always thank your assistant coach for their help at any training session or game and when given chance be sure to praise them at meetings, presentations, and in write ups in the local press.

As head coach you have to be prepared to, if necessary, let your assistant go. If you find out during the season that they aren't right for the team you can't just let them go on, even if they are volunteering their services it doesn't mean they can't be gotten rid of. If you are having problems with the other coach it will show and have a negative affect on your attitude and a negative affect on training. You need to be able to go to each training session and match solely concentrating on what needs to be done instead of having to wonder about your assistant.

What some coaches who don't have assistant coaches do is to bring in guest coaches from time to time to work on specific things and to freshen up training sessions. Players seem to have more respect for coaches that come in on a one-off basis and are more willing to listen to them than their coaches they see every week. The idea behind guest coaches is that if there is an area of your teams game you want to work on but don't feel you are the best person for the job then you can get someone who specializes in that area in.

Before hiring your assistant be sure to check their qualifications. Do they have a coaching certificate and a police safety check? Ask about their experience and where possible try and ask some other people that have worked with them about them. I know this isn't the Premiership but with the current climate we live in you have to be sure of who you are taking on - you can't just let anyone coach your players.

Coaching Family Members

In TV there is a rule to never work with children or animals. In youth football you could change that rule for family members but if you did hardly any teams would get off the ground. A lot of teams are started or kept going by parents who just want a team for their child to play in. Parents set teams up for many reasons. Some will set up a team if there isn't a team for their child. Some if they aren't getting on with another club. Some will do it because they want to help control their child's footballing career.

Coaching your own child can be very hard. Now doing one-on-one coaching with your own child is easy when you are down at the park, but when you have to look after the coaching of a team as well as your own child it is a completely different ball game.

As a parent coach regardless of how you treat your own child compared to the other players in your team the other players and their parents may always think that you are showing favouritism to your own child. There are coaches who will do this, make their child the captain, and have them as the striker who everyone else has to pass to and who never gets subbed. This is only one side of the coin though as some coaches will be that worried about parents and players accusing them of favouritism that they will be tougher on their own child than anyone else to make an example. Their child may always be the first to be subbed, never made captain and get more telling offs than anyone else in training.

If you do treat your child harder than anybody else you have to explain to them why you are doing it as if they don't know why, it can affect your relationship with your child as if you ask most children who play for their parents they don't want to be treated any different to their team mates. You also have to consider things like how you address each other at training and how to deal with problems when they arise. For years you will have built up a relationship with your child and you will interact in a certain way then all of a sudden to ask your child to go in to a player coach relationship and then back in to a child parent relationship outside of football can be difficult to do.

A big problem can come if your child is getting bullied by another player in the team as it then becomes hard for you to be objective. Your natural reaction is to look after your child and even if you do handle it objectively you may get other players and parents complaining because as you are a parent of a child involved they won't think you are being objective. This is why you need an assistant coach or a close link with your club committee so they can handle situations like this because as a parent you are in a no win situation.

If you don't have a child on the team you coach you will only usually see your players at training or at games but when you are a parent you will have your child talking to you about football and the team away from training. They will tell you what they think is going right or wrong which is sometimes a bad thing and sometime a good thing. You may at times as a coach have confidential or matters of a private nature relating to other players on your team which can be hard to keep private with your child in the house so that can become a struggle. There are also other things that you may not want your child finding out about like team selection for the next match because they might go blabbing it around the team. Your child will also invite other players over to the house or go to visit them so you will also be in regular contact with other players.

Young players who have a parent as a coach can have problems getting accepted by the rest of the team so it is important to do all you can to integrate your child. If a player has a problem with the coach they may take it out on the child of the coach, if they don't think the coach is doing a good job they will tell their child. The child then has to put up with all of this and then has to decide on whether to tell their parent or get on with it as if they told their parent it may get them annoyed and want to quit coaching.

The child will also become a messaging service for you as the parent coach. This is because they will see the other players in school and in the local area so they will pass messages to you through them.

The main thing to remember if you are a parent coach is to not let if affect your life as a family away from football. In football, try not to expect too much from your child and to always be supportive. Let them have free choice and not feel forced in to playing because their parent is the coach. Don't take it personally if they want to leave the team or join another team. Be fair to them, don't treat them better than other players in front of the team if they aren't, but never put them down. Your child has got to want to play football and enjoy it.

Counsellor, Childminder, Mentor, Friend and Parent all Rolled in to One.

As a coach at times you will have to be all these things to your players. When you build up a good relationship with your players they will start coming to you with all their problems which you will have to deal with. When working closely with young people you can't just expect to come and coach football.

At football you will see your players at their best and at their worst throughout the season. No matter how many times you tell your players not to bring their problems to football and to leave everything outside of football young people have problems doing this. If you just happen to be the first adult they see and that they trust after a problem has happened they will more than likely come to you for support.

After seeing your players for a few weeks at training you will get to know their individual personalities and how they behave. As you see them on a weekly basis you will be able to spot their mood swings and when they are acting out of character. It is hard for a young person to keep up a shield for a whole season so normally you are going to be able to tell when something is up.

The problem with noticing when something is up with one of your players is that some will want to come to you for help and some will want to keep it to themselves. As a coach it is important that players know they can come to you but don't have to if they don't want to. Never pressurize your players into having to talk to you about their problems. Your time spent with them should always be about football, only breaking from that if they ask you to.

Your players will come from a range of backgrounds and experiences. Some will have a so-called better life than others but it doesn't mean that all young people can't have problems. As a coach it is important to be aware and sensitive to the situations your players find themselves in but to try to not treat them any differently because of it. If you ask young people what they want to be most will say they say just wanted to be treated normally.

A key thing to remember is to always ask for help and don't keep things to yourself as a coach. You have a duty of care for the wellbeing of your players so if a player discloses something to you, you need to pass that on to the right person or department. No matter how much you want to win and keep the trust of your players if they tell you something which you fail to report then something bad happens people are going to ask you why you didn't speak up earlier.

It is only natural as a coach to build up friendships with your players but you have to remember at all times that you are the coach and they are the players. Try not to have contact with your players outside of games and training to keep that distance. Not only is it best practice but if you don't do this the player may come to you with all their problems which is not productive and is not your job as a coach to deal with.

Never get in to a one-on-one situation with a player. If you have to deal with a player in a one-on-one basis always make sure you do this in a public area which is overlooked by other people. This is for your own safety as well as the safety of your player. Don't exchange email addresses or other personal information with your players. When you need to get hold of your players try to go through their parents where possible.

As a coach be someone that inspires and motivates young people. Use your life experience to try and help your team of young players achieve on and off the field. Help guide them and mentor them to achieve the most they can with their lives. Give them support and confidence which enables them to play better and do better in life.

Some parents will see the football team as a child minding service where they can drop their children off and pick them up at the end. This is the basis of your job as if you do nothing else whilst you have them for football you have to mind them and look after them. Some parents would be more than happy with you offering advice and support to their children but some would rather that was left up to them so always be careful when dispensing general life advice to your players. Never try and replace their parent or act as if you were their parent.

Every child in your team will come from a different background so never try and judge what their life is like outside of football. Never pay too much attention to anyone player or treat them as special. Don't play favourites, everyone in your team should be treated the same with the same amount of time given to each player. Some of your players will need football more than others because of what is happening with their life outside of football so you will always get players who want to be there more than others but this shouldn't change how you deal with them. Most players don't want to be treated differently because of what is happening in their life away from football. They just want to be part of the crowd and part of the team so treat them as such at all times.

As a coach don't be afraid to instil discipline in your players and to show them right from wrong. Reward good behaviour and help those behaving badly to see the error of their ways and change their behaviour. Remember above everything that you aren't their parent - regardless of what it may feel like at times. You are merely in charge of their care for that hour at training, or for the time at a football match.

When dealing with players always follow the clubs rules and procedures. If you are unsure of how to deal with a situation speak to your club officers and get the guidance you need. As a coach you are never going to know how to deal with every situation so if you are unsure of what to do don't just try and figure it out by yourself - that's what your club is there for.

Getting Emotional

As a coach you are going to get emotional, it's the nature of the job. We're all human and it is hard not to get caught up in the emotion of youth football as a coach. The one thing as coaches we have to remember is that we are supposed to be setting an example so you have to try and keep your emotions in check at all times.

There is no feeling like when your team wins and I think that a lot of coaches are in the business because of this feeling. As a coach you will feel so happy to see your players achieving and to see them happy about their accomplishments. As a coach you just need to make sure that the result of a weekend fixture doesn't affect your mood for the rest of the week. You can't let what is happening with the team overwhelm you life outside of football. Coaching is something you do as a volunteer; as part of your life, not as your whole life.

When your team loses it is hard not to be upset, angry, or annoyed on the inside, but it is important that you don't show this on the outside as your players will usually be disappointed enough without you adding to it. Never take your frustrations out on your team as it will only make things worse. Shouting at a team after a defeat isn't going to help morale or turn them into a winning team. Then again, don't take the disappointment of losing in to your life outside of football and let it affect your day-to-day life. Always try and find the positives and think of proactive ways of dealing with a loss, learning from it, and making your players better players.

At training it is very hard not to get wound up by your players when they are messing about and pushing you to your limit. It is very important that you don't react to them. Most of the time they will be trying to get a reaction out of you and if you give it to them they win. At training you can't let the behaviour of a few affect how you treat the whole of the team. In training you have very little time so you can't waste any by getting stressed or annoyed.

As a coach you're going to have good weeks and you're going to have bad weeks. Some weeks you will come home wondering why you bother at all and you are going to feel like chucking it in. In these situations you have to go back to thinking about why you are doing it. You have to remember that nobody is putting a gun to your head forcing you to be a coach. If your heart isn't in it then you are doing a disservice to your players by being there. They deserve to have a coach whose heart is in it and you should contemplate relinquishing your position if it isn't. Coaching should be something you do because you enjoy it. The moment you stop enjoying it should be the time you think about calling it a day.

No matter how badly behaved a team is you will know in your heart if the team is worth your effort and if there is hope for them in the future and hope for you to turn it around. If you came in to coaching to make a difference in young lives then a badly behaved team shouldn't be a reason to quit, you should see it as a challenge.

Even in youth football at some teams there seems to be immense pressure to win games, to win leagues and to win cups. These teams will analyse every result in their league and work out how each result could change the table. They will use the results to assess how good or bad they think the opposition for the next game is and pass all this information on to the players telling them that the game is a "should win" game if they think the opposition isn't very good or a "must win" game if it is against someone near them at the top of the table.

As a coach it is ok to research these types of things yourself in your own time but you shouldn't be passing on that pressure to your players. Every game should be treated like any other, by saying "should win" and "must win" you put extra pressure and stress on to the players. If you say these things and the team loses it can bring even more disappointment to them than if it had just been treated like a regular game. Again this is another bad part of the professional game which is creeping in to youth football. If there are jobs or there is money riding on a game then it may be a must or should win, but this should never be the case in youth football. Your players need to be free of stress and pressure to just go out and enjoy playing their football.

Whatever is happening in a game you need to keep your emotions in check. If you are losing you can't show your disappointment to the players as it is your job to keep them positive. If they see you getting depressed then it is only going to make things worse. Young players have enough trouble dealing with defeat or going a goal behind in a game without you adding to it. It is ok being disappointed on the inside, it's human, but you have to keep that feeling inside.

If you are winning you have to try and not get too carried away. Yes show you are pleased with what your team is doing but you need to keep your players focused. Nothing hurts like taking the lead and then going on to lose the game. If you let your players get carried away after scoring a goal this can easily happen. You need to convey the importance of concentration and to show them that you don't want them to take their foot off the gas or to show them that they still need to keep it tight at the back and not go all out on attack. It is up to you to keep your players feet on the ground and to keep them respecting the opposition and the threat on the pitch.

When a game is tight you have to try to not show you are anxious or stressed. The players will be feeling the stress enough without you adding to it. The moment you go out of control is the moment your team will start getting out of control. Not just the players, but the parents also need to see that you are in control as if they think that you aren't they may take their child out of the team. They won't want their child in the care of someone who they don't think is in control.

When things are going wrong don't start blaming other people. It is easy to lash out at people like the referee during the game but doing this only makes your players think it is acceptable to do the same. You need to keep a level head when things are going wrong and look at how you can change your team or your tactics to readdress the situation.

Showing that you care about your team and how you do isn't a bad thing, it's a good thing. If the players don't think you care then they may start to not care themselves. However you need to do this in the right way and at the right time. You always need to lead by example and be able to put things in to context. Football should be something which is an emotionally beneficial experience for your players. Players need to experience losing and how to deal with it and players need to get that emotion of accomplishment from winning as it may inspire them on to do even greater things but you have to let your players experience this in the right way, a positive way.

Being the Best You Can Be

As a coach you should always want to learn and become better. As the team grows you need to grow with it as if you don't the team may outgrow you.

After every coaching session and training you should be able to objectively analyse your performance and look at what you need to change and improve. If you don't feel like you can be objective get some one who you trust to give you feedback. When you get that feedback be sure to take it on board and do something with it.

As a coach you can always improve and develop. The moment you stop wanting to do that is the moment you start going backwards. Sometimes it only takes experiencing a real situation to improve but sometimes you can improve without having to have an experience, so don't wait every time until you experience something in coaching to change your ways. It's like sometimes you only truly know what you would do as a coach when you are in the heat of the moment and faced with the situation. It's easy to say what you would do if a certain situation arose but actually having to deal with it is a different kettle of fish. It's like if a spectator was being abusive; you know you should deal with them, but would you have the nerve to go over to them and sort the situation out? Learn from every experience you have and even if you didn't handle it right the first time put it down to experience and remember it for the next time.

Take time to look at how other coaches in your league are coaching and see what they are doing differently. As a coach you have to be your own person so I am not saying that you should copy somebody else but don't be afraid to take ideas you like from other coaches and weave them in to your own style.

As a coach you have to adapt to your team - your team shouldn't adapt to you. As a coach you are there first and foremost to get the players playing the best they possibly can be, not adapting to your style of coaching. If your way of coaching gets the best out of the players then do it but if it fails to do so then you have to change. If you want long term success as a coach you need to be versatile.

Always try and get as many qualifications as possible. I'm not saying qualifications make you a better coach necessarily but what they do show is that you have committed yourself to coaching and learning. You never know when those qualifications may come in handy as they may unlock doors and positions that you wouldn't be able to get without those qualifications.

Read a lot about coaching and psychology. I often find myself reading books written by coaches as well as books on psychology as I am always looking to improve myself and the way that I coach. I also like to watch DVDs with drills and training techniques on as well as football matches on TV. If you search the internet you can find a ton of books and DVDs related to football coaching and training. Some will be helpful and relevant, while some won't be, it's up to you to try and figure out which ones you think will be useful.

Your players train to play football so you should train to coach. If you are unsure of how to do a drill, practice it before training, get some players together, set it up, and trial it. Do the same if you have come up with some new training techniques. Don't wait until training night and hope it works out. If it doesn't it will waste time and make you look like you don't know what your doing which won't win you the players confidence. Always have a plan before a session and evaluate how it went afterwards. On top of weekly plans you need to have long-term plans of what you want to achieve with the team, and of how you want to develop as a coach so always keep them in your mind and tick them off as you go. Sometimes based on uncontrollable circumstances your plans might go out of the window and you may need to think on your feet, but this will be the exception and not the rule. You should be prepared for it and able to deal with it, but it shouldn't stop you from creating weekly plans.

Treat every training session and game as a new challenge. The moment you start getting lethargic is the same moment that your players will and the moment your coaching goes downhill. Your job as a coach is to enthuse players - keep it fresh for them. If you think training is getting boring there is a good chance that your players are finding it boring as well.

If you don't feel confident going straight in to coaching try your hand as an assistant coach to someone who you know is a good coach. If you are working under a good coach you can learn good habits and get that all important experience. The only problem is if you are working under a bad coach and don't realize this you can pick up bad habits which are hard to rectify.

If a training session goes badly don't get down about it. All coaches make mistakes and have bad training sessions or bad games; the key thing is to learn from it and change it for next time. When something goes wrong always work out the reasons why it went wrong and then deal with them.

Your career progression as a coach depends on what type of coach you want to be. Do you want to stick with one team and take them as far as they can go, or do you want to get experience coaching as many different teams and age groups as possible? It's up to you what you want to get out of it. Most youth coaches stick with one team until they go into adult football and then some will then call it a day or some will then go on the lookout for another team to coach.

As a coach regardless of what's happening and what you are feeling on the inside always be confident. The moment you lose your confidence is when people will start questioning you, or your players will start playing up. If you give off a persona of thinking you are the best then the moment things go wrong will be the moment your coaching and your standing will be brought in to question. The best policy is even if you are the best coach in the land stay modest and let your coaching and your players do the talking for you. A good coach in youth football is judged on how many of their young players are enjoying it and how they have developed as footballers, nothing more.

Arguing Players

One of the biggest tests of your skills as a youth football coach will be when players fall out. If you coach youth football for long enough it's going to happen sooner or later. When this happens you need to be prepared for the situation and get it dealt with as quickly as possible. The longer a feud between players goes on, the bigger the problem becomes.

Young people will fall out and make up all the time. One minute they're best friends the next they're sworn enemies. As a coach you have to try and not get sucked into the drama that is the life of a young person as you will never be able to keep up.

As a coach you need to know when to let players sort out their own feuds and when to step in. When friendships break down between your players it can mean that players don't give their all at training, and could fear going to training as they don't want to see the person they are fighting with. In the worst case it will mean that a player won't come to training and you may have to field calls from the player or the player's parent about the situation.

The problem with only seeing your players for an hour a week and on game days is that it is hard to make changes and get a friendship back on track whilst trying to run a training session. Most of your players will fall out in the time outside of training when they see each other in school, or out in the local town, and you are powerless to stop it or do anything about it. Regardless of how good you are at keeping your players friends if they want to fall out they are going to fall out.

It is good to know before training if your players are fighting as you will be better equipped to deal with it. Some of your other players may tell you that some of their team mates have fallen out or you may get a parent coming up to tell you about it. When parents get involved it can become nasty as they are both supporting their child. They will want something done to protect their child, and they will normally think that it is the other child that is in the wrong. So unfortunately not only is it the players you have to sort out but the parents as well.

When things happen in football you need to stamp down on it there and then. If one of your players won't pass to another player you can pull them aside, or if a player doesn't want to pair with a player you put them in a pair with you can do the same.

A common problem you will have to stamp on is team mates making fun at the expense of another player. When they laugh at a team mate who messes up, or say nasty things about how bad they think their team mates are, these are things as a coach you can control and something you can't tolerate.

In your team you will normally have a player who everyone else aims to be like or be best friends with, a player who is seen as the cool kid. The problem with this is that it will breed competition between your players to become this person's best friend which doesn't bring out the players best qualities.

This is why building a good team harmony from the start is so important. You need a team of players who care about each and that support each other on and off the football field. Always make training as fun as possible and encourage players to work with different players at every training session. If you keep players working with the same players every week it only builds the feeling of separation between players in your team.

Try not to spend too much time during training dealing with squabbles. Sometimes the bigger the issue you make out of it the bigger the problem will become. Stamp on it when you see it and then spend time outside of training rectifying it or else you are paying a disservice to the players that come to training and want to play by spending their time sorting out other people's problems. Don't reward the squabbling players with more of your time and don't let the rest of the team suffer.

Feuds between individual players can turn in to team wars. If you have players in the team that have best friends in the team then if their best friend is squabbling with a player that means they have to join in. Even if this isn't the case, if two players are fighting the rest of the team will usually pick whose side they are on which will also divide the team.

Regardless of how good a coach you are there will always be players falling out. When players fall out it isn't a reflection on your coaching. How good you are as a coach is based on how you deal with players who have fallen out.

Paperwork and the Media

A lot of your time as a coach will be taken up doing paperwork. As with everything these days people are spending more time doing paperwork than their actual job and football coaching is no different.

For every player that plays a registration form has to be completed. For every game played a match report sheet has to be completed with a complete team sheet. For every postponement a form will have to be completed and so forth.

On top of this you will have the clubs forms to fill out which include things like these: an emergency contact sheet for each player, an accident report form, a payment of fees form, as well as various others. Besides the basics whenever there is an incident you may have to complete an internal report and if you meet regularly you might need to write a report for your meeting. Any paperwork you give to the players will normally have to be vetted by the club. This can be things like player contracts, fixture lists, and any notice about behaviour. When looking for players you may want to make some flyers for the local area and again these will need to be vetted by the club.

This is just the mandatory paperwork, no doubt you will also have your own paperwork including training plans, tactics, formations, notes, reports and all other coaching aids you can think of. This side of things can be as paperwork heavy or light as you want it to be. Personally as a coach I always like to write plans for training and games. Afterwards I will then write down my thoughts on how I think things went, which players are doing well in certain areas, and which players need to improve in certain areas.

You need to keep organized with your paperwork. Get yourself a folder and keep plenty of copies of all the forms you need so be ready to make many trips to the photocopier. If you are lucky your club may at the beginning of the season issue you with a folder containing everything you need.

Always try to do as much paperwork as you can before training and before games as you don't want to be wasting time at training or at a game filling out forms and if you are rushed you may complete them incorrectly. If you are trying to fill out a form which needs to be sent to a league you need to make sure you get it right as they could fine you if you don't complete it correctly.

With your own paperwork that you choose to do to help you coach, before the season starts try and make some templates to make it easier for you. I will always set out training session plans and game plans in the same way, so a template can save you a lot of time. Keep it organized and keep it consistent. Try to do as much of your paperwork on the computer as possible as if the information needs to be read by others it just makes it that much simpler and it minimizes the chance of someone misreading it or being confused by it.

Remember to always look after your paperwork. If you are at a game and it is raining keep your match report form in a folder, or in a plastic wallet either in the changing rooms or the car if you don't have changing rooms. If you try to submit a form which isn't legible because of the weather it could lead you in to trouble. Have a folder system and keep to the system. Always file your paperwork and if you ever have to send any of your paperwork off be sure to keep a copy for your records. When sending important paperwork you may also need to get it sent by recorded delivery - especially if it is a club or league matter. Leagues will ask you to send in paperwork on a pretty fast turnaround so the quicker you can get it done the better. Once you have been in a league for a while you will get used to the system and it will become second nature but if you are a new coach with so much other stuff to focus on you need to keep organized as things will quickly start going wrong if you aren't.

Good notes are important for training purposes, particularly if there are incidents in training and something builds up. If a child or a parent makes a complaint you need to have the whole story clear in your head detailing the events which lead to the situation. Doing this will also help you spot regular misbehaviour and may help you pick up on things you may not have noticed if it hadn't been for the notes.

Keeping good match notes can help you deal with the media. Most local papers will have a section for youth sport and your players and the parents of your players will like reading about their games in the local press. Normally the paper will have a cut-off day and time that you have to get match reports in for them to make print for that week. So when you get home from a game you then have to write your match report ready to send in. To begin with it can be quite tricky but over time you will get to know what your local paper likes and how to write for them. Sending in a match report isn't a guarantee that it will get in the paper; if it is a busy week it may get pushed to the next edition or not published at all so it can be a bit of hard work for nothing at times. However it is important to do a match report as when they do get printed it is good publicity for the club which is what you should always be aiming to create. A match report will also spread the name of your team about so you may get new players wanting to join and it may make it easier trying to get players to play for you. In a match report you can give special recognition to players that you thought did well and deserve the recognition, and it also gives you the chance to thank people like the sponsors if you have one as the sponsor deserves to get some publicity and recognition for supporting your team. Not only this but it can help you when looking for sponsors or when you are trying to raise funds as people who read the local paper will have heard of you or know you are looking for a sponsor.

If you have an assistant coach you can pass some of this responsibility off to them but with things like league forms as a coach the responsibility comes back to you so if you do leave it for your assistant you have to still make sure it gets done as if it doesn't get done and done properly it will fall back on you.

Politics

In many clubs you will have to deal with either real or perceived politics. It may not be the professional leagues but politics does exist in youth football. Politics is the reason that many people leave youth teams as it's everywhere from the clubs to the leagues.

Politics within clubs comes from when you have many teams sharing facilities, equipment, or funds. If you are in a club situation which has many teams where coaches start to see other teams getting treated differently they will quickly get annoyed.

Some politics are borne out of personality clashes between coaches and/or people on the committee. If somebody falls out with another person they will claim they are getting treated differently because of that personality clash.

In some clubs you may have members that say a lot about other club members behind their back and in some instances this can get back to the person they were talking about. In youth football for some reason instead of telling somebody to their face what you think of them, many people will act nice as pie to each other and wait to slag the other one off behind their back.

In the club you may get people that like to stir up situations. Some people will gleefully tell someone what has been said behind their back. Some people will even make things up or say things which aren't completely true to further wind up situations.

Politics isn't just confined to your club. Politics will be all around you, in other teams, leagues and local football organizations. In some cases if you are not liked by an outside organisation it will affect the way they treat you. Especially if these organizations have representatives from other clubs in your area.

The first thing you need to look at in the war on politics is your team. If you want to get rid of politics from your local football scene you have to lead by example and get your team right first. If you have politics within your own team it can make the weekly running of your team unbearable and may make you want to quit coaching.

In your own team you need to make sure everyone is treated fairly. Everybody needs to be picked for the team based on their ability and their effort and nothing else. Everybody needs to be given a fair chance to claim a place in the team and in a position which will give them the best chance of succeeding. As a coach you can't let one person play in a position they ask to and then not let another player play in a position that they asked to. You need to stay uninfluenced by your players' demands on that front.

You have to arrange days and dates of fixtures with the team in mind and not arrange things around one or two players. If you arrange things around one or two players it will show the rest of the team that you think those two players are more important than the rest of the players on your team.

In training you need to make sure you give equal attention to all your players and not just a selected few.

It's not just adults that can notice politics as young people can see it too, and if the parents notice politics within the club then they will become uncomfortable or even possibly take their child out of the team.

After you have eradicated politics from your own team you then have to look at the club. If you have problems with other people on the board make it your mission to work on it and sort it out. Go and talk to them and find out why people treat you in a certain way or treat you differently, then if they do tell you why and it is something you are doing try to work on it.

When wanting to try something new with your team or when you want to buy something new for your team always get the permission of the board. If you don't do this it could cause you problems as you will be seen as a loose cannon. Your club may have to rein you in and keep a closer eye on you which may cause more politics. The way to eradicate politics is to always do everything by the book and to do it the same every time.

Some people in your club may try and play the politics game to their advantage. They may try and get friendly with certain individuals within the club to get their own way and what they want when it comes to team and club matters. If someone else in the club sees what they are up to then the person playing the politics game will get a reputation in the club for doing it.

It is very easy to get caught up in the politics game without even realizing that's what your doing so you always need to be aware of how you are acting and how you are treating people. Regardless of what politicking is happening around you, you need to not let it change the way you act.

You need to be careful with your selection of assistant coach and then to keep a watchful eye when they are on board as they may start politicking behind your back. If they think they can do a better job they may be politicking behind the scenes to get their own team or even to take over the team from you. You need an assistant coach you can trust as you don't want to come to training every week wondering what they may be up to behind your back. If the parents of your players are on the club committee or friends with people on the committee you have to be careful of what you say to them as again they could be politicking behind the scenes to get you out. Now you can't live your life as a coach being paranoid about all these things as these things will only happen in rare occurrences but it is just something you need to be mindful of.

If you are joining a club which is already established then you need to work out the political situation at the club before you do too much as a coach. You need to learn how the set up works, whose friends with who and what the relationships are like between club members. If you don't do this and you open your mouth or do something before assessing the situation you can easily alienate yourself from certain people in the club. When starting in a club try and keep your mouth shut and you ears open, don't get drawn in to giving opinions on people and things within the club as if you say something which is seen by them as of out of turn it could get back to certain people within the club.

If you have a situation like this at your club you have three choices. You can either not let if affect you and continue regardless, you can try and do something about it, or you can look for a new club. If you aren't happy at your club it will show in your coaching and it may affect your attitude and mood outside of football.

Luckily there are some great clubs out there run by great people who treat the club very much like a family and whose aim it is to do everything they can to get young people playing football and enjoying it. Normally these clubs are hard to get in to as none of the staff want to leave but the good thing when you do get in to them is you won't want to leave either!

Getting Involved With the Club

When you run a team in a big club it is very easy to just think about your team and not to think about the club as a whole. A lot of your time will be taken up by your team and they have to be your first priority. However it is important whenever possible that you support the club.

If you need more money to buy things with for your team you can't expect not to help out or show your face for fundraising events and then expect to be given the funding by the club. You can't expect your club to keep you informed of everything that is happening and to be able to read your mind when you want something, so you need to keep in contact with other club members to know where the club currently stands.

If you want support from people involved in other teams whether it be coaches, referees, or parents you can't expect them to help you and drop everything if they don't know you or if you haven't helped them out. Another good thing about getting to know parents from other teams is that they may have other children who would be eligible to play for your team. Parents will have jobs or skills from their professional life which can help you out. Some may be teachers or some may work in the building trade so can help on ground renovations. The bigger the network of contacts you have the better.

A good thing about going to the games of other teams in your club is it can enable you to see if an opposition is cheating. Sometimes in some clubs players will play for a couple of the teams even if they are too old so if you have seen them playing for other clubs you can easily spot them if they come and try and play in a league or cup game against your team.

Going to look at other teams in your club can give you ideas. Different coaches will run things differently so you can get training tips, new drills and learn new tactics for game situations. As you have a pool of talented coaches at your club it makes sense to share your knowledge and experience as you should want all the other teams in your club to do well as it will enhance the name of the club as a whole.

Always make yourself accessible to other people within your club. If you try and keep your team to yourself and keep yourself at a distance from the club it may create a 'them and us' attitude which is not healthy for the club or your team. A lot of your paperwork and official matters will go through the club first before it gets to you so it can make it very hard to function without the support of your club and you're just making things harder for yourself.

It's always good to know if a team in your club is feuding or has a rivalry with another team in their league as if that club has a team in your age group that feud may spiral to your league as well so it is always good to know what is happening on that front.

Always make your players feel like part of the club and help them get to know players on the other teams. As a club you should stick together and the players should have the chance to make as many friends as possible. This can be especially important if you are coaching an age group that is going to move up to Secondary School as you can make their transition that bit easier if they already know people in the older teams who go to that school.

Building relations between the players is good for both them and you. It gives them more people who they can have a kick about with outside of training and a chance to learn something by playing with different players. It will also help keep them out of trouble on the streets and to help stop them from getting bullied. Players in all teams should be there to support each other and it should be the older players taking the younger players under their wings. A way you can push this is by having some of your players helping coach the younger teams or if you coach a younger side getting in some of the older players to help out from time to time. The players should know who else plays for the club and at the very least know them to say hello to.

As a coach try and volunteer to help the club as much as possible. There will be lots of work which goes in to the running of the club but if enough people do their fair share then you can divide the work up nicely so it isn't as much of a burden. The club works to help your team play football so it is only right that you give something back.

Presentation Evening and Rewarding Your Players

All season you will be hard on your players in an effort to keep them disciplined. Trying to keep your players focused all season is a hard job. This is why Presentation Evening at the end of the season is so important. These are run by the club and most clubs will have one, if they don't try and get one arranged. This is an evening where regardless of where your team finished in the league that you can reward them for their efforts and hard work to make them feel like they achieved something this year. It's also about the players getting recognition in front of their parents, other parents, their team mates and their peers the players from other teams within the club.

Presentation Evening is also a night which recognizes the team as a whole and is a time where you can share the achievements of the team with the rest of the organisation. As a coach you can say a bit about how the team got on and how well individuals did. It also gives you time as a coach to publicly thank anybody or any organisation that has helped you through the season.

At some Presentation Evenings coaches and volunteers will get awards and get recognition but you have to remember the night is about the players. Normally at a Presentation Evening the players will each get a memento or trophy to keep which recognizes their participation in the team. This is great as no matter what happens the players always have something to look back on in later years as a memory of the season. It's important at the end of the season to get all the players from your team together like this as you don't know who will be going or staying next season.

On top of this you will give out individual special awards to members of your team that have gone that extra mile. Examples of these could be manager's player of the year, team player of the year, most improved, top goal scorer, and players' player to name just a few. These awards may vary from club to club. The players' player award will be voted on by the players so that is a special award as it is your team mates recognizing who is the most deserving but for the other awards it is up to the coach or coaching staff to select the winners. This is of course also except for the top goal scorer award which is based on the amount of goals scored in the season. This will be the only award that players know who has won before the presentation evening starts.

For the awards where you as a coach have to select the winners it can become very difficult to choose who should win each award. If you could you would give every player a special award, so picking a handful of players from your team can be like having to pick between your own children.

When selecting who should win which awards you have to take a lot of things in to consideration like who won the awards last year and how to spread the awards around or else you will have one player winning everything. If you are a parent coach you have to make a hard decision as some coaches won't pick their own child for an award as they don't want to be seen to show favouritism or if you do pick them you have to be ready for other players and parents to think you are favouring them. As a player if your parent is the coach and you know they go out of their way not to show favouritism you may think you may never get an award but if you do get an award you will know you deserved it. On the opposite side if your parent gives you an award you know you don't deserve then it can feel like a hollow award and not well deserved, or if the player doesn't think like that they may be oblivious to what is really going on and think they are the most deserving player when they are not. So parent coaches will have an even bigger headache with this one.

With the managers' award you will be looking for qualities like reliability, someone who listens and does what you tell them to do and someone who always gives one hundred percent for the team. This award shouldn't be about who the best player is because if you do this then a lot of the team would be out of the running before you have even started. For team players you will be looking for the person who always does everything for the team, really motivates them and picks them up when they are down, someone who leads by example. Most improved can be a difficult choice because your players over the season will improve in different ways at different things. Players' Player which is voted on by the players will normally go to who is the most popular on the team.

Presentation Evening is normally a good publicity event as well as you can get the local press down to take photos. Getting award photos in the paper is great as it is further recognition for the players for their hard work and shows the club rewarding their players. Photos like this can encourage new players to join the team for the next season. Different clubs will have different dress codes for awards nights. Some will want the players to come in clothing from the club, some will want them dressed smart, and some will want them in their social clothes - it just depends on the club you are at.

Outside of Presentation Evening you can choose during the season when and how you want to reward players. This can be done through a simple man of the match award or you can devise your own awards and rewards system. Regardless of what you give players you should always reward players with praise when they do something right or do something well. This can mean a lot more than an award to some players and they will remember the words of praise for years to come and it will help their confidence and ability more than any award will do.

Leadership

As the coach you are the captain of the ship. It is your job to keep everything under control and in check no matter what is going on around you. During the season you may have to deal with many different things but it is your job to not let this affect the team and to keep it going.

It is your job to make sure the team complete the season and aren't forced to drop out or fold. You can't control the amount of players who may leave or quit the team throughout the season but it is up to you to make sure that a full team goes on to the pitch each week. When players leave it is up to you not to dwell on the players you have lost but to get in new players and to work with the players you have left to make them the best they possibly can be, changing tactics and positions if needed.

If results aren't going your way it's up to you to keep the team going, to keep spirits up and to keep the team together. It's up to you not to throw in the towel and to pull the team out just because they are losing every game. If you do that it teaches the players that it is ok to quit when things aren't going your way. You should never start a team unless you are going to see it all the way through to the end of the season. You have to be ready to experience the worst. If you do pull a team out it can give the club a bad name or hinder anyone else's chances of starting a team at that age group in the area.

As a coach you are responsible for everything that happens within your team and you have to be accountable. When incidents happen it's up to you to sort it out and to not sweep it under the carpet or to try and avoid the situation. You have to deal with every situation or complaint.

It is up to you to take the pressure off your team in pressurised situations - like when you are in a cup final or need to win your last game to win the league. No matter how pressurised you feel in a situation you need to make sure you don't pass it on to the players.

As a coach you need to be able to make your players believe they can achieve anything and have no fear when going in to a game. You have to make believers out of them when they go in to games and you have to inspire them to go that extra mile. Being a great leader is about getting a performance out of a player that not even the player thought they were capable of. Even if you feel inside that the opposition is a better team or that you are going to lose in a match, you have to make sure that your players don't think like that and that you don't show that on the outside.

During a game if you think you have conceded too many goals and that there isn't enough time to get them back you can't show that to your players. They will probably already be thinking like that but you need to motivate them and get them playing to the end believing that they can still get something.

As a leader you need to set your team and players achievable goals and targets that they can reach. You as the leader need always to have a goal of what you want the team to achieve and keep everyone on course to reach that target.

In leadership you need to be able to keep your players feet on the ground and not let them get complacent. You need to make sure your players are prepared to work hard for every victory and to know that each victory won't come easy. It is important that you don't let yourself get caught up in the hype and the excitement that comes with achieving a string of victories.

To be a leader you need to stand up for your team. When people are saying negative things or untruths about your team you need to stand up and fight for the good name of your squad. Players like to play in a team which has a good reputation. If the team is getting ridiculed they may leave the team as they don't want to be thought of as a bad player or playing in a bad team. Your players may not feel brave enough to stand up for the team so you need to step in. You need to also teach your players how to deal with people who are being negative towards the team.

As the leader of your team it is up to you to build confidence in your players. When your players are confident it gives them the ability to deal with people being negative towards the team and to not let it affect them. It helps remove fear when they go out on the pitch and it makes them welcome a challenge. You need to also help build players confidence in each other. Players need to have the confidence in each other to always pass to who is in the best position and not to who they think the best player is. They also need to trust that each player is going to do their job on the pitch and do it to the best of their ability whether that be making the tackles in defence or scoring the goals up front.

Building appreciation within your team is an important job for a leader. You need to make sure that all your players appreciate each other and don't take what they do for granted. If they start taking each other for granted and just expect them to do things then some players may leave as normally most players don't mind playing out of position or playing in a different way than they are use to just as long as they are appreciated. If your players start falling out on the pitch or blaming each other for things that are going wrong then that is your fault as a leader for not building a better harmony within the team.

You need to always remember that you are there to be the leader of the team and not a friend of the players. If you are there to be friends with players and parents then you will start making decisions based on friendship and not on what is right for the team.

Being a good leader is all about being able to make the unpopular decisions and to have the strength to be unpopular if it is for the greater good of the team. If you're only interested in being liked by your players, parents and other teams then you can never be a good leader.

For the Love of the Game

Through all the ups and the downs of youth football it is your love of the game that makes it all worthwhile. The love of the game is what makes all the stress, the tears and the time spent on it worthwhile. If you don't love what you are doing then you will only get upset and annoyed by it, causing you to either be a bad coach or to quit coaching.

There is nothing more rewarding than seeing your players having fun and to know that you were involved in making that happen. With so many bad things happening in the world and with all the problems young people go through whilst growing up to see them doing something they truly enjoy is a great feeling.

Seeing young people change and develop in front of your eyes is such a buzz. Instilling confidence in a player that didn't have any to start with is amazing as this is something that will have an affect on that young person's life and help improve their life outside of football.

Great football coaches don't just want to work with the best players. The great coaches enjoy taking players who may not be considered good or may not have kicked a football before and turning them in to great players. They love working with players who no one else has been able to coach and to turn them in to great players. They are also the ones who can take on the challenge of a badly behaved player and turn their behaviour around. You can have the best team in the world but if they aren't getting any better or improving then you have failed as a coach as that is what your job is.

Football will give you so many memories and experiences that will stay with you forever. It's not the wins or the trophies that you remember it's the games where your team overcame adversity or gave their best performances that you remember. The days where you had to travel a hundred mile round trip and play in torrential rain are the memorable ones. There are situations which you get in youth football which you would never get in the professional leagues and it is these situations which make it great.

If you wake up on game day hoping that the game is going to be called off then you haven't got the love of the game or when you don't want to go to weekly training you haven't got the love of the game. If you are not enjoying coaching you will stop going that extra mile and trying to get away with doing as little as possible. The problem is when you start doing this your team's attitude and performance will reflect yours so you are doing your team no favours by staying on as coach.

The only way you can enjoy and succeed in coaching youth football is if you have the love of the game. If you don't have this then every little annoying thing is going to become unbearable and depress you. When things start going wrong you're not going to care, not try to make the difference and just accept it.

You are never going to be a perfect coach or the best coach in the world but it's about being the best coach you possibly can be to your players. If you always want to get better as a coach and to do more for your team then you are in the right job. Being a youth football coach is a calling which you either have the personality and attitude for or you don't.

Coaches with a love of the game think of and treat their team as if they were family. They care for their players' wellbeing on and off the pitch. When they go home from training they will be thinking about how they can improve or change things. You know you truly love what you are doing when you are at work or at home and you are thinking about your team.

Being a youth football coach takes so much of your time and your energy that you need to be committed to it. You will need to make sacrifices and have time during the week which is set aside for football and where you can concentrate on that and nothing else. You should not let your personal life away from football affect the way you coach or lead you to pass on your problems to your players. You need to be able to push all that to one side and forget about it whilst you are coaching. Players should not know or be able to figure out what is going on in your life as you need to keep that separate. You are there to help them and not to bring them down or for them to help you with your problems.

You need to always make sure that as a youth football coach that you are doing it for your players and your team and not just for what you get out of it.

Final Thoughts

Coaching youth football is one of the greatest things I have done with my life. It is so rewarding to see first hand the difference you are making, there is absolutely nothing like knowing that you played your part in helping somebody. I must say though that coaching youth football is not for everyone.

As I have explained through the book something which you would think would be so simple like coaching youth football can be at times anything but. The book is a warts-and-all look at everything which happens in youth football. The book is here to prepare for you anything that could happen to you but it doesn't mean that it all will. Many coaches go through their coaching life not experiencing some of the issues and problems I have addressed in this book so don't let it put you off.

Reading through this book you may think coaching youth football is all doom and gloom but even if you have to deal with all these problems the positives which you can and will experience always outweigh the negatives. Your job as a coach is to be aware of all the things I have addressed in the book but to not let them affect you in a negative way.

Being a youth football coach is truly an important job. Some of your players may not listen to their teachers or their parents but they may listen to you. Through sport you can achieve so much with young people and teach them valuable lessons which they can't learn anywhere else.

Only get into youth football coaching if you have the time. Young people have enough people in life that don't believe in them or don't have the time for them so you need to make sure you are committed to them. If you can't make training or matches ninety nine percent of the time then you need to let someone who can be committed run the team as young people need that commitment and to not feel abandoned.

Coaching youth football isn't just for those people who want to get in to professional coaching. People who want to get in to professional coaching are normally just coaching a team in a local youth league as a stepping stone to the next stage of their career. Young people need coaches that are going to stick with them, a coach that is going to make the team their number one priority and not their career. In youth football you can't always do things the way that football organizations tell you to do things like some coaching drills on a professional football DVD, this is where you need to be able to change and adapt things. This is something a coach looking to go professional may not be willing to do as it may go against what they have been told.

You don't need to be or have been the best footballer to be a great coach in youth football. To be a great coach in youth football you need to be able to work with young people, the ability to make things fun, the ability to get the most out of people and the ability to be a great leader.

The best coach isn't judged by the results their team gets or the standard of players they have. The best coach in youth football is the one who has made the most positive difference in the lives of their players and only you know if that is what you are trying to achieve. Some times you may never know what effect you are having on your players or find out what effect you had on them but you always have to try every week to do this in the hope that you are making change.

Youth football is never boring and there is always a new challenge around the corner. Just as you think you have your players and your team figured out something or someone will change and you will have to start over again. Sometimes you may feel like you are part of a soap opera or teen drama with the things which will go on throughout the season as there will never be a dull moment. Just when you think things have gone quiet, things will start kicking off again, but you won't want it any other way.

There is always more you can do, and there is no limit to what your players can achieve. So if you want a challenge, want to make a difference and see young people change and develop in front of you then being a youth football coach is the job for you. There is nothing on earth quite like it to me. For to me, actually being a youth football coach is a better experience than anything you see in any of the sporting movies or TV programmes.

Printed in Great Britain
by Amazon.co.uk, Ltd.,
Marston Gate.